BONUS ONLINE CONTENT

Entrepreneur MAGAZINE'S

ULTIMATE
GUIDE TO

Social Media
MARKETING

- Get a 360-degree look at social media marketing
- Craft a social media strategy that gets your business seen
- Engage with the right audience and build a following

ERIC BUTOW, MIKE ALLTON, JENN HERMAN, STEPHANIE LIU, AMANDA ROBINSON

Entrepreneur Press, Publisher
Cover Design: Andrew Welyczko
Production and Composition: Eliot House Productions

This publication is designed to provide accurate and authoritative information in regard to the
subject matter covered. It is sold with the understanding that the publisher is not engaged in
rendering legal, accounting, or other professional services. If legal advice or other expert assistance is
required, the services of a competent professional person should be sought.

Entrepreneur Press® is a registered trademark of Entrepreneur Media, Inc.

Library of Congress Cataloging-in-Publication Data

An application to register this book for cataloging has been submitted to the Library of Congress.

ISBN 978-1-59918-674-0 (paperback) | ISBN 978-1-61308-432-8 (ebook)

Printed in the United States of America

25 24 23 22 21   10 9 8 7 6 5 4 3 2 1

Contents

Foreword

by Andrew & Pete, founders of andrewandpete.com

Guess what. Social media isn't the new way to market your business. Nope, it's not.

In fact, calling social media the new way to market your business is like saying Amazon is the new way to buy your Christmas presents, or even better, that Maroon 5 is this new up-and-coming band that is going to be huge.

Want to feel old?

Did you know Maroon 5 won the Grammy for Best New Artist the same year Facebook launched? Bonus points if you know the year.

Social media isn't new; marketing your business on social media isn't new. This isn't a fad—it's here to stay.

In 2019 we walked onto a stage in front of 5,000 of our peers.

The stage was at Social Media Marketing World 2019 in San Diego, the world's largest social media marketing conference. We were the closing keynote on day one. Before a backdrop of palm trees and surfboards, we told the audience all about social media marketing success stories and how businesses and brands are thriving online, like fitness guru Joe Wicks, who now has more than 100,000 customers, thanks to the power of social media.

Or what about the UK TV show *Love Island*, which went from a "failed concept" to the country's most watched digital TV program in 2018, thanks to the show's savvy use of social media marketing.

Every day we see brands like Burger King, Spotify, Wendy's, and Charmin, to name a few, connect with their customers in new and inventive ways that get them trending, while other brands like JD Wetherspoon and Lush get roasted for failing to talk to their customers on social platforms.

So whether you're a big brand, a small business, a TV show, or a blogger, social media can't be ignored.

But social media can be a few other things, too:

- It can be like your last relationship . . . complicated.
- It can be like your in-laws . . . a little hard to bear sometimes.
- It can be like the Kardashians . . . hard to keep up with and remember who's who.
- It can be like your favorite TV show that got canceled on a cliffhanger . . . Really. Blooming. Annoying.

Because here's the thing: Social media isn't new, but in a lot of ways it is. Social media is a little Maroon 5 mixed with a little Billie Eilish. It's old and it's new—all at the same time.

Because although a lot of the social media platforms have been around for what seems like forever, the features, capabilities, and what you can achieve with social media change on a daily basis.

So that's why it's good that you have this book, because as the title suggests, this is the *Ultimate Guide to Social Media Marketing* (it's best if you say that in your head in a really epic voice, with an emphasis on the *ULTIMATE*).

If you want to know how to grow your business, using the not-so-new-but-still-ever-changing social media landscape, then this book is for you.

If you don't like writing in the margins of a fresh-smelling book, we recommend grabbing a new notebook, buckling yourself in, and getting ready.

EPIC VOICE TIME: This is the ULTIMATE Guide to Social Media Marketing.

Enjoy.

P.S. It was 2004. There's no prize, but fist-bump if you got it right.

Preface

Trying to keep up with all the changes in every social network within a printed book is as futile as going to the ocean and keeping the waves back with a broom. To float on with this metaphor, it may seem as if the number of social media marketing services is so vast that if you use all of them, they'll wash over you and drown your business.

Ultimate Guide to Social Media Marketing takes a different approach by showing you how to decide which social media platforms are right for you and use them strategically to drive more customers to your business.

You're not the only one who thinks social media is vital to the success of your business. Buffer's "State of Social" 2019 survey reported that 89 percent of company marketers say social media is very or somewhat important to them. Seventy-three percent of respondents also said that social media marketing is somewhat or very effective for their business.

What's more, a March 21, 2019, study by business website The Manifest, "How Small Businesses Use Digital Marketing Channels in 2019," showed that 73 percent of small businesses invest in social media marketing, which is tied with websites as the top digital marketing channels for small businesses.

According to the Buffer survey, only 49.1 percent of companies have a documented social media strategy. If your company is part of this 49.1

percent, this book will help you refine your strategy so you can get even more business. If your company is part of the 50.9 percent that don't have a social media marketing strategy, we'll help you put one together.

WHAT TO EXPECT IN THIS BOOK

Here's a high-level overview of what we'll cover in this book:

- *Why businesses need to embrace social media marketing.* To the casual user, social networks are about connecting with friends and keeping up with today's latest trends and trending topics. In business, however, you need a strong sense of how social media marketing fits into your overall marketing strategy, especially the roles of content and email.
- *Understanding today's social networks, from big ones like Facebook and YouTube to emerging platforms.* You need to know the nature of each social network, including the types of content that can be shared, how audiences are grown, and what the typical demographic is. Once you know the nature of different social networks, you'll know which ones your business should be on.
- *Learning how to craft your business's social media strategy using today's formats.* We'll not only tell you how to craft your social media strategy, but we'll answer some important questions as well. Do you know the difference between a link post and an uploaded video? Do you know the requirements and restrictions for posting on different social networks? We'll answer these and other questions so you're not caught off-guard.
- *Using images and video in your social media outreach.* You need to include images and video in your social media posts to communicate effectively with your customers. We'll tell you how to source images and video as well as use them strategically.
- *Leveraging chatbots, paid social media, and influencer marketing.* These three features of social media marketing are very effective at growing your online community, and we'll teach you how to use each feature on different platforms to drive customers to your business.
- *Building your business social marketing team.* Your time is limited, and if you want to spend your time serving customers rather than managing your social media, you need to outsource tasks to another business or hire a full-time employee. We'll tell you about the key considerations you need to build your team effectively.
- *Measure your social media outreach progress and improve your performance.* Social media success is not measured by likes or comments. Instead, it's an ongoing experiment to see how well your messages resonate with your audience. So we'll show

you the best ways to approach social media analytics, how to determine your real business ROI, and how to adapt and improve your message over time.

In sum, this book takes you through a 360-degree perspective of social media marketing, from strategy to tactics, from organic to paid, from B2B to B2C. It encompasses all the current social media networks, from the large ones like Facebook and LinkedIn to emerging platforms like Snapchat and TikTok. We've also included a list of useful resources and a glossary of terms for easy reference.

Before we dive in, however, you should have a good picture of what is and isn't social media. That's where we'll begin in Chapter 1.

The Power of Social Media

The need for human connection is right smack in the middle of Maslow's hierarchy of needs, and has been a psychological truth of our species for ages. Humans have a deep-rooted desire to be part of communities where they are accepted and have opportunities to contribute.

As far back as the 1960s and 1970s, with the advent of early computer networks, there were glimpses of how that need for connection would be transformed into digital relationships and online platforms.

Remember the days of dial-up modems? Those happily beeping 2400-bps magicians were incredibly slow by today's standards, but their affordability and portability made it possible for even the most basic home computer to access online servers.

By the mid-1990s, the early social media platforms were born, starting in 1997 with Six Degrees, where you could create a profile and foster relationships with other people online. Friendster and MySpace brought new levels of features and capabilities in the early 2000s, and shortly after we were off and running, with LinkedIn and Twitter and Facebook. Figure 1–1 on page 2 gives you a brief look at just how quickly the social media companies you're familiar with popped up.

Network	Launched
LinkedIn	2003
Facebook	2004
YouTube	2005
Twitter	2006
Pinterest	2010
Instagram	2010
Snapchat	2011

FIGURE 1–1. Today's social media landscape

All these platforms share two common traits:

1. They help individuals find and connect with other individuals, fulfilling a basic psychological need.
2. They were *not* designed for businesses.

Facebook and LinkedIn even have features called Groups where anyone can create a community around an idea, issue, area, theme, or brand, allowing members to connect and discuss common interests with one another.

And, of course, people today use social networks for news and entertainment as well. Gone are the days when they rely on a daily newspaper or the six o'clock news. The networks often provide trending news topics and stories, and people can rely on their friends and connections to share the most talked-about posts.

While most network founders intended to "monetize" their platforms in some way, be it through display ads or something else, their initial goal was to help people connect in some new and unique way.

YouTube, for instance, was created simply as a way for people to share videos with other people. At the time, other social networks did not support video playback, so YouTube was unique. Within a year, it was growing at a record-setting pace. Video advertising, which played before user-uploaded videos, is a monetization concept that launched *more than a year after YouTube was founded*.

This kind of post-launch implementation and constant evolution of social media is why businesses find it challenging to come up with a successful, clear social media strategy. It's ever-changing and unclear and nuanced. In many respects, traditional advertising is easier. Take billboards, for example.

A business can work with an advertising company to identify one or more billboard placements that seem promising, due to location, traffic volume, or some other factor.

They'll hire a graphic designer to create the perfect vinyl artwork, which the advertising company installs, and then negotiate and pay a set monthly rate according to their contract.

That's pure advertising. Your business, along with countless others, adopts a "Pick me!" attitude and hopes to get a potential customer's attention long enough to make a lasting impression. And in many respects, it works. The right billboard (or radio spot, newspaper ad, or TV commercial) at the right time in front of the right person can absolutely drive business results. But it's expensive, impersonal, and challenging to measure.

There's no way to know how many people looked at your billboard, or even gauge with any certainty how many people drove past it. Traffic estimates are based on municipal studies, which are conducted infrequently. And of course there's no way to have a conversation with the people who look at your ad unless they reach out to you first.

Contrast that with social media, where businesses can create profiles for free, share content and information for free, and freely review metrics and reports provided by those same social networks, which detail exactly how many people saw and engaged with their business online. That, coupled with the ability to use Google Analytics (also free) to measure referral traffic to a website from social media, offers businesses an incredible opportunity.

How to approach and leverage that opportunity is of course what the rest of this chapter and book will address. We're going to cover the importance of relationships and creating connections on social media.

BEING SOCIAL ON SOCIAL MEDIA

Because every social network is, first and foremost, designed for individuals, businesses are at a distinct disadvantage. Adopting the "Pick me!" broadcast approach isn't just ineffective; it's likely to backfire. While people have been conditioned to accept the existence of ads online, there is tremendous animosity toward businesses that want to interfere with the primary reason they're on these social networks.

In other words, people use Facebook to connect with their friends and family, not your business.

Rather than present you with a list of technical requirements or some arbitrary definition to determine whether an online service counts as a social network, what's important is that you understand the underlying meaning.

Does the online service facilitate the connection of individuals and the development of relationships? If so, even if it features a fraction of the users of Facebook or Twitter, it can safely be considered social media for your purposes. That means sites like Yelp or Flickr or Pinterest have their place, though some may argue over the nuances.

The important take-away is that people use social networks to connect with, talk to, and learn from other people. If, as a business, you can insert yourself into that process and help them fulfill that need, you'll be on your way toward a successful social strategy.

As motivational speaker and marketer Jay Baer put it, "Focus on how to be social, not how to do social."

This means that to be effective at social media, businesses need to know how to build relationships. That's admittedly hard because relationships are formed one person at a time. Businesses that are already large, or in a hurry to become large, may be more enamored with ideas of scale and rapid growth.

Social media works very similarly. When someone follows you or comments for the first time on a post, it's an opportunity for you to welcome them, virtually, to your storefront. Will you rush into your sales pitch, or take a moment to encourage some dialogue and attempt to build rapport?

Fortunately, Chapter 10 is going to help you tremendously: it is in fact possible to scale relationship-building by using influencers as a bridge and conduit for relationships with customers.

HOW ONLINE RELATIONSHIPS BENEFIT OFFLINE

Before you get rolling with influencers, however, it's critical that you and your brand establish your own presence, personality, and message. Because even if you're using social media and communicating with people as your brand, it should still be clear that there's a *person* behind the logo who's talking.

The benefit is that through the use of social media in a way that is eminently social, brands can build relationships with fans, followers, prospects, and customers that lead them to know, like, and trust that brand. And that often leads to tremendously valuable relationships *offline*.

Take the 360 Marketing Squad, for example.

Jenn Herman, Stephanie Liu, Amanda Robinson, and Mike Allton, four of the authors of this book, have a private mastermind group for mutual support, as well as a paid membership group for students who wish to learn digital marketing. The four of them enjoy deep, supportive friendships and a tremendously successful business partnership—all made possible through social media.

Jenn and Mike became acquainted on Google+ back in 2012, where Mike had established nearly a quarter-million followers and Jenn was launching her career as an Instagram expert. Over the years they supported each other and developed a friendship.

They met in person for the first time four years later at Social Media Marketing World.

Stephanie and Jenn first learned of each other through Instagram and Facebook. They both had developed tremendous reputations as internet marketers, finally meeting in person at Social Media Day San Diego in 2017. That same year, Mike and Stephanie connected on Instagram, and were later introduced in person at Social Media Marketing World 2018 by Jenn.

Amanda and Jenn have shared many mutual connections in their respective spheres of influence on Facebook and Instagram. The two of them would carry on their online conversations in real life each time they saw each other at Social Media Marketing World and eventually became great friends.

While at the Midwest Digital Marketing Conference that year, Mike and Stephanie talked about the importance of having a support group, a Mastermind, and thought it would be a great idea to start meeting with Jenn, both as online marketers and as the parents of young girls. Out of that trio was birthed the idea to create a paid membership group with rotating experts, but they needed a fourth person to complete the group. That's when Amanda was brought in, and the rest is history!

A strong support group and lasting friendships, a business partnership that generates five figures of shared annual revenue, a live show, a podcast, and now a book— all made possible thanks to social media and building relationships both online and off.

Your results may vary.

Here, these four experts on social media marketing, with established expertise on every platform, are joined by co-author Eric Butow, who has written dozens of books on marketing and technology. Together, we represent decades of experience in every facet of online marketing and are bringing it all to bear for your benefit.

Throughout the rest of this book, we will be diving deep into specific networks and offering strategies and tactics that you can employ and adapt to your own business. Take notes, develop tests, and always consider how what you're doing can help develop relationships and contribute to the online *experience* that your fans are participating in.

Chapter 2

Understand Today's Social Networks

Social networking websites are much like any other human social constructs—each website requires different behaviors and has different expectations of its participants. Visiting each social network can be like being in a different country. People on Facebook will expect you to behave very differently from people on LinkedIn. (If you're looking for a different analogy, you may find Jenn's comparison of social networks to martinis amusing in her article at https://bit.ly/2uZdHZe.)

The risk of including a list of social network websites in a book is that one or more of them may have vanished by the time you read it—lost in the ether or bought by another company. Do you remember Friendster? Vine? Google+? Yes, even large, competent companies like Google can get social networking wrong.

We decided to include ten social networks not only because ten is a nice round number, but we also thought these social networks had the biggest and fastest-growing user demographics when we wrote this book in early 2020.

Before we dive in, keep some things in mind about the information in this chapter.

All demographic statistics are current as of September 2019. We largely took our information from two sites that regularly monitor social network website usage, eBizMBA and Omnicore Agency. You can visit these sites at your leisure for the latest and most complete demographic information; we have limited demographic information in this book to the points we think you'll find most useful. (Friends don't let friends get analysis paralysis.)

You'll notice that in this chapter we talk about how some social networks are more interdependent with other social networks. Yes, that's because these social networks are owned by other networks. In particular, Facebook owns WhatsApp and Instagram but allows them to operate independently (kind of like the suburbs of a large city).

Two other social networks are owned by large companies: YouTube is owned by Google and LinkedIn is owned by Microsoft. So we'll talk a little about how these social networks interact with other tools offered by these companies.

Chances are you have many colleagues, if not friends, who want to follow you on the social networks you're using. So, you have to get out the social network version of a fife and start playing to let them know where you are. (We know your friends and colleagues aren't rats . . . not that there's anything wrong with that.)

Even if you're already using social networking websites, take stock of the other ways you're connecting with your contacts and see if there are opportunities to invite them to follow your social network profiles. Examples include:

- Your email signatures
- All your email newsletters
- Your websites and/or blog websites
- All other social networks you use
- All pages you use on social networks, such as a business page on Facebook and/ or LinkedIn

If you want to check your connection methods right now, do so. We'll wait here until you get back. Once you've chosen new ways to include your social networking icons, you can decide where to add them, such as in the sidebar of your website. We'll talk more about using social network logos correctly in Chapter 5.

This chapter not only briefs you on each of the ten networks' user demographics, but you'll also learn about the types of content you can add and how you can grow your audiences in each network. Then you'll be ready to learn how to build audiences for your preferred social networks, starting with Chapter 4.

FACEBOOK

Facebook is a lot like Walmart. Just as Walmart has become the de facto "general store" in the United States, Facebook (see Figure 2-1, on page 9) has become the de facto online meeting website for everyone around the world. Consider the following demographics:

- Facebook has 2.2 billion unique monthly visitors. (That's not a typo.)
- The country with the most Facebook users isn't the United States—it's India, with 270 million users. The U.S. is in second place with 190 million users.
- Of all the people who connect to the internet, 83 percent of women and 75 percent of men use Facebook. However, when you split Facebook users by gender, 57 percent are male.
- Most Facebook users (96 percent) use the Facebook app to access Facebook sometime during their day.
- Facebook skews to a younger demographic. Eighty-eight percent of web users age 18 to 29 use Facebook, and 84 percent of online users age 30 to 49 use Facebook. Even so, 72 percent of online users age 50 to 64 use Facebook. And 62 percent of users over age 65 use Facebook, too.
- The average Facebook user has 155 friends.

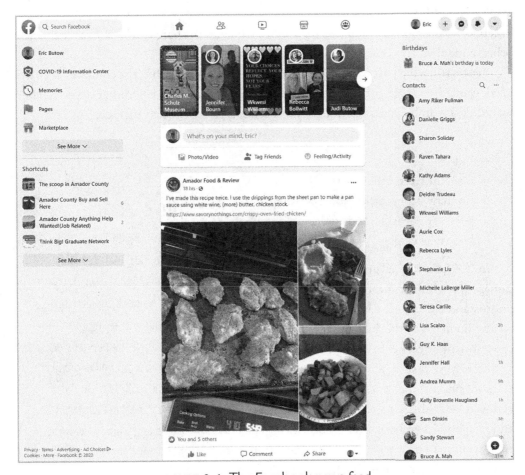

FIGURE 2–1. The Facebook news feed

Many people, including Facebook executives, realized long ago that having so many users on one website was an opportunity to make money. Facebook offers a number of ways for businesses to advertise on the site, including creating pages and groups as well as paid advertising. Here are some convincing reasons why businesses advertise on Facebook:

- Seventy-five percent of online users who have $75,000 or more in income use Facebook.
- As of 2019, Facebook had more than seven million advertisers, and we're willing to bet dollars to doughnuts that number is higher now.
- Facebook's share of the entire global digital ad market is 19.7 percent.

Do you want to learn more before you commit to a strategy? Then put your bookmark right here and get the full scoop in Chapter 9.

What Can I Share?

Facebook was originally designed for college students to share text messages with each other, and (obviously) the model took off from there.

Text is still a big part of sharing information on Facebook, but the company realized users wanted to share other types of content as well, and if they didn't allow it, they wouldn't stay in business very long. Those other types of content include:

- Photos
- Videos
- Content from other users
- Content from other sources, such as blog posts, podcasts, and video blogs (better known as vlogs)

In 2017, Facebook upped its game by adding a camera app within its mobile app so users could take photos and videos. All you have to do is tap Photo on the homepage and then tap the Camera icon in the upper-right corner of the Camera Roll screen.

After you take a photo or video, or add one or more photos and videos from your camera roll, you can add them to another feature Facebook added in 2017: Facebook Stories. Stories let you add effects, animated "stickers," and geolocation tags to your photos or videos. Geolocation tags let you

TIP

You may be thinking, "Hey, that sounds a lot like what Snapchat does." You are correct: Facebook copied what Snapchat was doing (and continues to do) after Snapchat declined its $3 billion buyout offer in 2013. Later in this chapter, we'll tell you what Snapchat is doing to combat this threat to its business.

TIP

Followers are people on Facebook who receive your posts in their newsfeed when they view your profile and click the Follow button. They may not want to be friends, or vice versa. However, if you're following someone who follows you, that's a good sign you should send them a friend request.

tell viewers where your photo or video was taken; you can specify with place names or latitude and longitude coordinates.

You can publish your photo or video with all your sparkly stuff publicly or send it as a direct message to one of your friends. If you post it publicly, Facebook deletes the post from your profile after 24 hours.

Make Your Garden Grow

Facebook gives you control over who sees your posts. You can publish a post that everyone on Facebook can see, or one that only certain people, such as your friends and followers, can view.

If you're the type of person who wants to have as many friends and followers as possible, which is especially likely if you're trying to promote your business on Facebook, here's a to-do list to help get people engaging with you and your posts:

- Authenticity in your posts will attract more views. That means you not only need to talk like a real person, but you should also post photos and videos you took yourself—don't use stock photos.
- Video gets more attention than images. They don't have to be long; start with 30-second to 60-second videos and see how they work.
- Write original posts most of the time, not just links to your websites or other social network sites.
- Don't overwhelm people with posts every day. Focus on quality over quantity and keep testing your messages and your timing to learn what topics get the most likes and eyeballs.

Some of these requirements may seem more obvious than others, but we've tried to be as thorough as possible because we know the old saying about the word "assume."

LINKEDIN

You're likely in business, so LinkedIn is our second stop on our tour of social networking websites.

TIP

This tells you how to grow your friends and followers organically—that is, for free. If you want to grow your following by paying for Facebook ads, then it's time to get out your bookmark, put it here, and read Chapter 9 before you return.

LinkedIn, which is shown in Figure 2–2 below, is the place where business owners, managers, and employees congregate online; it's also a popular place for job seekers to find work. Here are some statistics to back up those claims:

- LinkedIn boasts 675 million users.
- The average LinkedIn user makes $46,644 per year.
- Fifty-one percent of college graduates in the United States used LinkedIn.

FIGURE 2–2. A typical LinkedIn user homepage

The LinkedIn Marketing Solutions Blog also published some good statistics in 2019 to convince you that LinkedIn is a place where you should market your business to customers:

- Ninety-four percent of B2B marketers use LinkedIn to distribute content, which makes it the top online B2B marketing platform.

- Ninety-one percent of marketing executives cite LinkedIn as their top online social network to find quality content.
- Ninety-two percent of B2B marketers include LinkedIn as part of their digital marketing efforts.

Market Effectively . . .

LinkedIn has a different audience from other social networking websites, so you should tailor your posts and your marketing appropriately. Here are some general guidelines to start with:

- Complete your LinkedIn profile because people want to know everything about you. LinkedIn has a useful profile builder to help you get and keep your profile up-to-date.
- Though you should be personable, you probably shouldn't share highly personal content like videos of your cat.
- When you write posts, talk about topics relevant to your industry or common business issues such as managing employees.
- Add images or videos of individuals to your posts when you can because visual posts get more interest than plain text. However, if you take photos of partners or clients, be sure to get their permission before posting them.

. . . But Don't Spam

As you make new connections, you'll notice that people will send you private messages selling their business or services, seemingly within minutes of accepting their connection request. It's up to you to determine if you want to remain connected with someone whose only interest in you is a potential sale.

It's important for you not to be a hard sell, either. You may have better luck using the pull method—that is, provide helpful information to as many people as possible, both in your industry

TIP

If you notice that LinkedIn promotes Microsoft products and services a little more often than those of other companies, that's because Microsoft bought them in 2016 for $26.2 billion. You can also link your Microsoft accounts to your LinkedIn account by opening the LinkedIn Settings & Privacy page, clicking the Account tab, and then clicking the Change link to the right of the Microsoft entry in the Settings list.

TIP

LinkedIn also allows you to copy your LinkedIn posts directly to your Twitter feed. However, if you write a post in LinkedIn that's longer than 280 characters, Twitter will cut off the message automatically, so keep that in mind as you write.

and in business generally. That information can appear in your posts and/or published articles. LinkedIn also offers groups about many subjects that you can join and participate in by writing your own posts and/or commenting on other members' posts.

Over time, people will become more interested in what you have to say and will check out your profile. You'll also make more quality connections (the LinkedIn equivalent of Facebook friends).

If you feel that you need to sell as hard as possible on LinkedIn, you can always pay to advertise your business. All you have to do is log into the LinkedIn website (not the mobile app), click or tap on Work in the upper-right corner of the webpage, and then click Advertise in the sidebar that appears on the right side of your screen. LinkedIn will take you step-by-step through setting up your first campaign.

> **TIP**
>
> LinkedIn also reminds you about important things going on in your connections' lives and invites you to connect with them to congratulate them or wish them well. Consider taking advantage of these offers to congratulate your connections with short public and private messages, because they'll help you keep your connections over time.

YOUTUBE

YouTube primarily lets users share videos and brief text descriptions with all YouTube visitors. Google saw the potential of YouTube right away as it grew rapidly and bought YouTube in 2006 for $1.65 billion. That turned out to be a good investment, because as of May 2019 YouTube had two billion unique monthly visitors—second only to Facebook.

Consider these other features of the YouTube user base:

- Ninety-five percent of the world's internet population watches YouTube.
- Fifty-one percent of YouTube users visit the website every day.
- Sixty-two percent of businesses have YouTube accounts they use to share video content.
- Seventy percent of total watch time on YouTube comes from mobile devices.
- Millennials (born between 1981 and 1996, according to the Pew Research Center) prefer YouTube two-to-one over traditional television. Generation Z (born from 1997 on) prefer YouTube by over three-to-one, per YPulse's 2019 "Media Consumption Monitor" survey.

When you open the YouTube homepage, you can watch videos based on your past viewing history, as shown in Figure 2–3 on page 15. You can share your videos on your

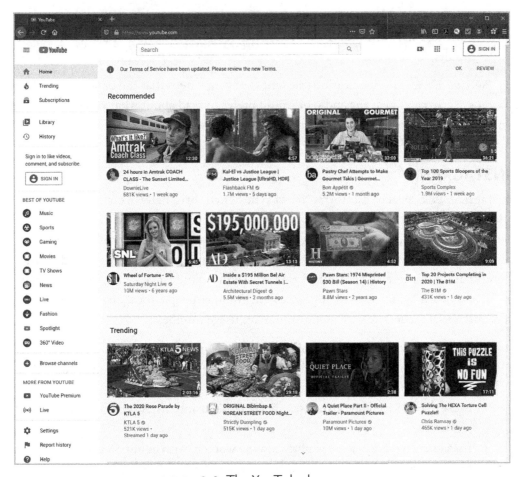

FIGURE 2–3. The YouTube homepage

YouTube channel, embed a link to a YouTube video from your website, and copy links to those videos to post on your other social network profiles.

If you've had videos created professionally or think you can make them by yourself with your phone, and you want to start a YouTube channel (if you haven't already), here are some simple guidelines to follow before you start:

- Watch videos produced by the best in your industry so you can imitate them.
- Provide content that educates, entertains, or ideally both.
- Test your content with other people, such as employees and/or friends, to see if the video delivers the impact you want.
- Add a title and a brief text description to your video that includes links to related websites, if any. Adding text to every video you post helps viewers understand more about the video and entices them to keep coming back to your channel.

- Ensure the title and description include search keywords. When users search for those keywords, there's a better chance they'll find your video in the search results.

What's more, consider creating transcripts of your videos that can be shared as a link so people who can't hear the audio or would prefer to read about what you offer can do so. It's all about serving the customer as thoroughly as possible, right?

INSTAGRAM

Instagram is a visual platform. It was designed originally as a photo-sharing platform, and while you can now post videos as well, all posts must still have a visual component (see Figure 2–4 on page 17 for a typical Instagram profile). You can't simply upload a text update or share a link. You must post a photo or video (or a combination of these as a "carousel post"), to which you can add text in the caption.

Though Instagram skewed largely toward younger people for many years, it is now a robust social media site with some impressive usage numbers:

- Instagram boasts more than one billion active monthly users (which puts it only behind parent company Facebook and its family of messaging apps, and You-Tube for most users on social media).
- More than 25 million businesses are currently using Instagram for branding and marketing.
- Instagram typically skews slightly toward women, with about 56 percent of users being female.
- Speaking of those "younger" users, 72 percent of teenagers currently use Instagram.

From a marketing and business perspective, Instagram is a powerful tool. You obviously have those one billion active monthly users to think about! But in addition to that:

- More than 200 million people visit at least one business profile a day on Instagram.
- Every month, 130 million users tap on a shoppable post to learn more about a product or to make a purchase.
- Instagram is a hotbed for influencer marketing and provides brands with more ways to connect with new and potential audiences.

That makes Instagram particularly viable for brands, especially those with an ecommerce element.

FIGURE 2–4. An Instagram profile layout

The Different Components of Instagram

For a "simple" photo-sharing platform, Instagram actually has multiple components you should be aware of. We'll break these down a little more, but let's look briefly at the regular home feed, Instagram Stories, and IGTV, where you can create or view content.

The Instagram Feed

The Instagram feed is what you see when you tap on the home button (the house icon) on your menu bar. This feed is full of content from the people you follow, any hashtags you follow, and any ads that have been selected for you.

This content is always a photo or video, or a carousel, which contains up to ten pieces of content and can be a mix of photos and videos.

TIP

People on Instagram are typically interested in visual content and want to see "pretty" images or videos. Posts with a lot of text typically don't perform well. Busy images that lack a focal point can be distracting, encouraging people to scroll right past the post. Instead, focus on creating quality posts that are well-formatted for color, alignment, and focal points.

Instagram Stories

We talked a bit about Facebook Stories earlier in this chapter, and Instagram Stories are very similar—except there's even more to do in Instagram Stories! That's because Stories were available on Instagram before Facebook began offering them. So there are more stickers, features, and interactive components within Instagram Stories.

Instagram Stories continue to gain popularity with users and are favored for their short-form content. Videos can be up to 15 seconds long, and photos appear for six seconds. And, like Snapchat, all Stories disappear from the user's profile after 24 hours. All this content is being viewed by more than 500 million users every day!

To access Instagram Stories within the app, you can swipe right from the home screen and the Stories interface will appear (on desktop, there's a sidebar block). From there, you can take a photo or video or use the Create feature to write text on a colorful background or generate other fun posts like shout-outs, quizzes, and polls.

All Instagram Story posts are a vertical 9:16 orientation, so photos and videos can be cropped, pinched, or arranged to fit within that space.

Instagram Stories are designed to be fun and interactive. They can have text, doodles, and stickers and are not meant to be heavily polished. If you're using Stories for your marketing, you'll want to keep this in mind for your content strategy.

IGTV Videos

Instagram launched IGTV in June 2018. It's technically a stand-alone app that you can download outside the Instagram app, but you can also view and access IGTV videos from within the Instagram app by tapping on the TV icon.

Standard IGTV videos can be anywhere from 15 seconds to 10 minutes long. Business profiles with more than 10,000 followers can upload videos up to 60 minutes long via the desktop. And similar to Stories, these videos are designed for a vertical 9:16 format, but other formats can be supported.

Advertising on Instagram

As we mentioned earlier, Instagram is owned by Facebook, so its advertising opportunities are as robust as the Facebook ads platform—because they're the same! You can access your Facebook ads manager to create and run Instagram ads as well. Some of the advertising goals and audience targeting options are slightly different, but Instagram is still a very good platform for running highly targeted ads to your ideal customers.

Instagram feed ads are the most common type of advertising, but Stories ads are gaining in popularity as well. IGTV ads are not widely available at the time of publication, but are expected to become so in the near future.

TWITTER

Twitter (see Figure 2–5 on page 20) acts like a social news ticker—it gives you brief information about what the people you follow are doing. Twitter limited its posts, or "tweets," to 140 characters at first, but in time it allowed users to add photos (still and animated) and videos to their tweets. In late 2017, Twitter expanded its tweets to 280 characters.

The popularity of Twitter among celebrities, politicians, journalists, and other movers and shakers keeps people coming back to the platform, which manages 330 million unique visitors worldwide every month. But Twitter isn't just about celebrities—executives, companies, and the rest of the world also use the service often:

- Forty-two percent of all Twitter users access it every day.
- Thirty-eight percent of Americans age 18 to 29 use Twitter.
- Fifty-six percent of Twitter users make $50,000 or more per year.
- Seventy-nine percent of all Twitter users reside outside the U.S.
- Eighty percent of Twitter users access the service on mobile devices.

FIGURE 2-5. A typical Twitter feed

Twitter offers businesses the opportunity to advertise, just as on Facebook and LinkedIn. However, if you want to grow your Twitter feed organically, beyond the standard social networking advice of posting valuable, original content, here are some things you can do to keep people interested in your feed:

- Keep your posts as short as possible—that's what Twitter is all about.
- Use Twitter as your first source for making announcements about your business.
- Add hashtags (for example, #2021planning), so people searching for topics in your industry will be more likely to find your posts.
- Consider posting every day: say hello, give a brief update, and ask other users what they're doing today. That post can be text, a short video, or both.

- Retweet someone else's tweets if you think they would be of interest to your readers. However, don't do it often; people will lose interest because they're not reading anything about you.
- Twitter gives you the ability to create polls, so get your readers involved by asking questions and getting their feedback through votes and comments. Consider your questions carefully, though: If a topic is considered too controversial or shocking, it may adversely affect your business, not just your number of followers.

Don't just use Twitter to promote yourself. You should also follow your competitors, influencers in your industry, and companies you want to emulate to see how they keep their followers engaged. Then you can imitate what they're doing, such as using similar hashtags.

WHATSAPP

As Facebook grew, it kept an eye out for potential competitors and moved to buy them as quickly as possible. That didn't work when Facebook tried to buy Snapchat, so they copied what Snapchat was doing instead. Facebook had better luck when they purchased Instagram in 2012 and WhatsApp in 2014.

You can make voice and video calls in WhatsApp, which makes it similar to Facebook Messenger or an instant messaging/phone call app like Zoom. WhatsApp (see Figure 2-6 on page 22) has 1.5 billion users in 180 countries, which makes it the most popular messaging app in the world. If you live in the United States, you may be wondering why you've never heard of it. That's because relatively few Americans—if you call 23 million people a few—use it.

If you want to learn more about WhatsApp, here's some useful information from the Business of Apps website:

- WhatsApp has 200 million more users worldwide than Facebook Messenger, which you may be more familiar with if you're in the U.S.
- One billion people around the world use WhatsApp daily.
- India boasts the most WhatsApp users in the world, estimated between 200 million and 300 million.
- WhatsApp users send 65 billion messages per day.
- Users also spend more than 33 million hours making voice and video calls in WhatsApp every day.

Like Snapchat and Facebook Stories, the WhatsApp Status feature allows you to share text, stationary and animated photos, and videos with your contacts. These Status updates disappear after 24 hours. What's more, you can share WhatsApp Status posts to Facebook and other apps.

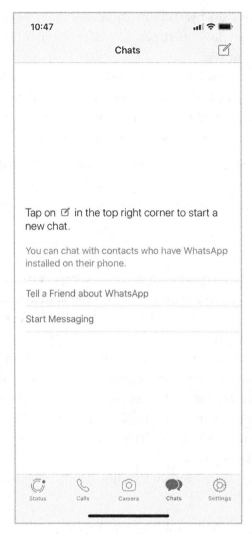

FIGURE 2-6. The WhatsApp homepage on an iPhone

If you're already working with international customers in your business, chances are you're already using WhatsApp because that's what your clients are using. You should download WhatsApp and start working with it if you plan to expand your business internationally so you'll be up to speed before you enter an overseas market.

PINTEREST

Pinterest is another social network that started in the late 2000s and found immediate success with its focus on sharing images more than text. The Pinterest login web page shown in Figure 2-7 on page 23 illustrates how photos appear on the site.

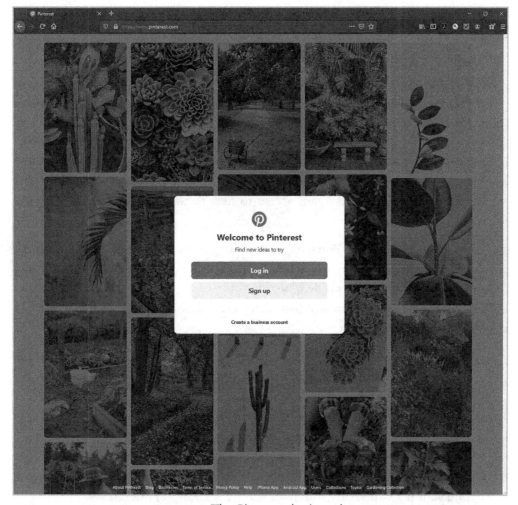

FIGURE 2–7. The Pinterest login web page

As of this writing, Pinterest has a user base of more than 250 million people that skews heavily to the female demographic:

- Women make up 71 percent of Pinterest users.
- Forty-two percent of adult women in the U.S. use Pinterest.
- Eighty percent of U.S. mothers who use the web use Pinterest.
- The majority of active users on Pinterest are younger than 40, which isn't surprising considering 34 percent of U.S. adults ages 18 to 29 use Pinterest.
- Half of Pinterest users earn $50,000 or more per year.

That last bullet point is of particular interest to both businesses and Pinterest. Pinterest also offers its Pinterest Business website so companies can promote their goods and services to these high earners.

So what are the differences between Pinterest Business and "regular" Pinterest?

- When you create an account, Pinterest Business lets you enter the name of your business in its entirety instead of separate first and last names.
- You can create Rich Pins that include pricing information and a link to your website to make pins even more valuable to viewers. (You'll learn more about Rich Pins later in this chapter.)
- Pinterest Business tracks and shares statistics of how every pin performs.
- Businesses can advertise by turning a pin into an ad, creating ads in different formats, and creating ad campaigns.
- Pinterest Business users gain access to new features before regular Pinterest users.

Whether you want to use Pinterest Business or prefer the original site, the rules for posting on it are slightly different. For one, Pinterest calls your posted images "pins" and organizes them into categories called "boards."

Once you have the terminology down, keep the following tips for using Pinterest in mind:

- Decide on themes for the boards you want and what pins you want to put in each board before you start adding pins.
- Pinterest is optimized to show photos in portrait orientation, so post portrait photos whenever possible.
- Just as with any other social networking website, make sure you take the photos you pin to show that you're authentic.
- Keep any text brief, but include keywords so current and potential followers will find your pins when they search for those keywords in Pinterest.
- Don't inundate your followers with a lot of posts in a short period of time. Instead, make a schedule and decide what you're going to post and when.

If you're promoting your business, then search for "Rich Pins" within the Pinterest app or website. As the name implies, Rich Pins are enhanced pins that allow you to add more information than just the usual brief text. For example, you can add pricing information from your website (if applicable) as well as your business name and logo in the pin description.

Pinterest Business also offers analytics to its users so you can find out what types of pins are popular with your audience over time. Not only will this tell you what pins you should focus on, but it will also guide you to any new boards with similar themes to your profile. All you have to do to open Pinterest Analytics is click Analytics in the top-left corner of the screen and then click Overview. Pinterest will guide you through the process of verifying your website. After Pinterest verifies your website, you can use Analytics to analyze to your heart's content.

SNAPCHAT

When it launched in 2011, Snapchat was the first app to allow you to add animated graphics and captions to your photos and videos and then have those posts disappear after 24 hours. Snapchat became and is still popular with many young people (disappearing posts help keep nosy parents at bay), and 90 percent of Snapchat's 360 million monthly users are between 13 and 24 years old. Figure 2–8 below shows the Snapchat app on an iPhone.

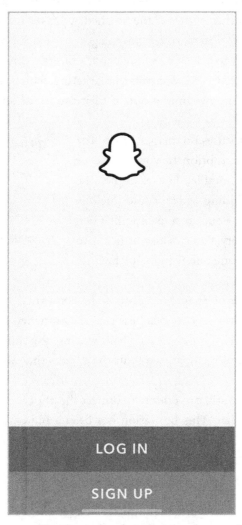

FIGURE 2–8. The Snapchat home screen on an iPhone

What's more, 41 percent of teenagers in the United States say that Snapchat is still their preferred social network platform even though Instagram Stories has copied Snapchat's form and function (and had the gall to use the same term for posts that Snapchat originally coined).

Snapchat has been working to bring more businesses into the fold by offering advertising on the platform, but you can also grow your business organically on Snapchat by posting a series of Stories. That series should be like an online short story: You should have one or two Stories as the beginning, another Story as the middle, and the final one or two Stories as the conclusion. (And you thought all that English homework wouldn't be useful when you were a kid.) For example, if you make something like cupcakes and want to show the process, you could post videos of getting the ingredients, mixing, baking, decorating, and then show off the finished cupcakes in your final Story.

Don't forget to add stickers, which are images you place on top of your photo or video, and you may want to use some of Snapchat's filters to give your images or videos a unique look. You may have seen Snapchat's marketing, which shows people in photos with large eyes and a rainbow coming out of their mouth as an example of the filters you can use.

Though Snapchat focuses on images, remember that you can also add a caption to your photo or video, so make it memorable. For example, the caption in your concluding video could include your website address or your store location. When you finish creating a Story, you can also attach it to an email or send it to someone using your favorite messaging app.

TIP

Select your email app to attach your Stories to an email, or select your messaging app to include it in a text message.

Snap Inc., the owner of Snapchat, seems to be concerned enough about Facebook and Instagram taking away its core business that it's branched its technology offerings into . . . augmented reality sunglasses. As of this writing, the third version of Snapchat's Spectacles is available and includes two built-in cameras that allow you to take photos and videos.

For some reason, you still can't directly connect the photos and videos you take with the Spectacles to Snapchat. This limitation has been a big reason why interest in the Spectacles has been . . . less than spectacular.

REDDIT

Before the web consumed the world in the mid-1990s, people communicated online using bulletin board systems, better known as BBSs. A BBS had different messaging forums focused on various themes or topics. In 2005, Reddit built on the BBS foundation by allowing people to include images and videos in their messages.

But the operators of Reddit needed a hook, and they found that allowing readers to vote on messages within a forum (called a subreddit or sub) engaged them. Posts with more positive votes moved to the top of the subreddit and were more likely to be seen than posts with fewer positive votes and/or posts with a lot of negative votes.

The formula has become so popular that Reddit (see Figure 2-9 below) has 430 million unique monthly users and the site even wrested the title "front page of the internet" away from Yahoo! as the latter became less relevant to web users over time.

TIP

Just like the BBSs of old, you can create your own, anonymous username (what BBS users called a "handle") instead of your own name. If you have a company, your username can be your company name. However, if you decide to use a different username, that could bring even more adjustments to your marketing strategy than you expected.

FIGURE 2-9. A typical Reddit newsfeed

Reading Reddit Messages

You can search for a specific topic on Reddit by typing the name of the subreddit in the Search box. When you open the subreddit name in the results list, you can subscribe to it by clicking the green Subscribe button. The next time you log into Reddit, you can access all your subscribed subreddits easily.

As you read Reddit posts, you can express your approval by clicking the up arrow next to the post or disapprove by clicking the down arrow. The most popular posts appear at the top of the subreddit newsfeed. As you scroll down, you'll start to see posts that aren't as popular with other users.

Posting on Reddit

The advantages to using Reddit for your business are much the same as with other social media networks such as Facebook and LinkedIn. That is, you can:

- Read about what's happening with your competitors if they're on Reddit. (If they're not, that's an opportunity for you.)
- Start conversations and leave comments in subreddits related to your business so you establish yourself (and, by extension, your business) as a resource.
- Create your own subreddit for your company or your ecosystem, such as businesses within a geographic area.

Before you start posting on a subreddit, which is the name of the subreddit topic preceded with "r/" (such as r/socialmedia), it would be prudent to read the most recent messages in that subreddit to get a feel for the topics.

Next, read the posting guidelines on the right side of the screen. Each subreddit has moderators, who set the rules for that sub. For example, the r/science subreddit requires you to make sure any research you link to is less than six months old.

Reddit makes it easy for you to write a new message, submit a new link, and embed a video or image into your post. As with other social network websites, you should keep any videos short and your text as short and informative as possible. Doing so will give you a better chance of people upvoting your messages.

After you post, other users can vote on and comment on your message. Each comment can also be voted on, so the comments with the most upvotes appear first underneath your post. As with other social networking websites, trial and error will tell you which topics in each of your subreddits are of most interest to other users so you can focus on those issues.

TIP

Many posts have links that can make navigating Reddit a challenge because links don't automatically open in a new tab. If you click on a link to read an article, you either have to make sure you open it in a new tab, or press the Back button in your browser to get back to Reddit once you're done reading.

TIKTOK

The most popular and talked-about social network in 2019—and perhaps the second most controversial behind Facebook—is TikTok. Beijing-based ByteDance Technology Co. bought lip-syncing app Musical.ly in 2017 and merged it with its own lip-syncing app in 2018 to create TikTok. (TikTok is known as Douyin in China.)

Both TikTok and Musical.ly did much the same thing: allow users to make 15-second lip-synced music videos, add filters to make them more amusing and colorful, and then send them to fellow users. You can learn more about TikTok on its website, shown in Figure 2–10 below.

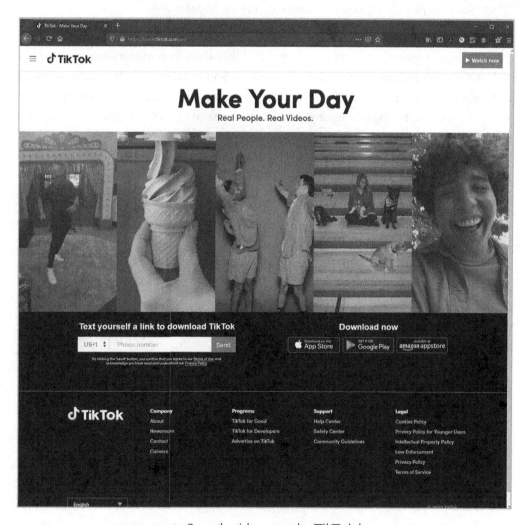

FIGURE 2–10. Sample videos on the TikTok homepage

ByteDance has continually upgraded the TikTok service, and its efforts are paying off—it now has 500 million monthly online users. The MediaKix website has some more interesting statistics about TikTok's rapid rise:

- People downloaded the TikTok app more than 730 million times in 2019.
- Only 26.5 million of the 500 million monthly online users come from the United States.
- The country with the most TikTok users is in India, which has 24 percent of all TikTok users.
- Though ByteDance is headquartered in Beijing, TikTok isn't available in China. The company still sells its original app there: Douyin.
- Sixty-six percent of TikTok's users are under 30 years old.

So when would you use TikTok to promote your business? If you want to attract young people, consider creating videos on TikTok in communities that dovetail with what your business offers. What's more, if you market your business overseas, particularly in South Asia, TikTok should be on your list of social media networks to review as you create your company's social media strategy. (You'll learn more about creating that strategy in Chapter 4.)

Creating and Sharing a Video

TikTok allows users to select from a wide variety of background music. Once they choose their music, they can use their smartphone camera to record themselves dancing and/or lip-syncing to the music. Once they finish capturing their video, they can edit it with a variety of filters, such as one that allows them to change the speed of the video.

When they're done editing, they can share it with other TikTok users or post it on YouTube and Facebook. TikTok is similar to those other two social networks in that you can set your TikTok profile to private and share your videos only with your friends.

What's more, TikTok has a variety of theme-based communities that you can search for. When you find some, view some videos in the community to learn what types of videos are popular before you record and post yours.

After you post your video, the users you share it with can use TikTok's "react" feature, which shows

TIP

If you're not sure what to create, you can open the For You page, which recommends videos based on what you've done in the app previously. For example, you may have liked someone else's videos, so it will show you other videos like that. Only users who are 16 and older can have videos posted in the For You page.

them reacting to your video in a small window in front of your video. That feature is an effective way to learn who likes your video within the community and/or within your group of TikTok friends.

Duets and Challenges

Two of the most popular features in TikTok are creating "duets" and "challenges." A duet is a video that is combined with another video so both videos can be watched at the same time. Someone can do this with your video and vice versa. If another user has the Duet feature turned off, then you can't add the video into your own duet. (You can also turn this feature off in your own profile or only allow friends to create Duet videos.)

You can also participate in a challenge, where one user will post a video about a topic and challenge others to post videos about that same topic. The One37pm website published a list of the best TikTok challenges in 2019; one example included showing off videos of a user's best artwork and a glimpse into their artistic process. This challenge created an atmosphere of creativity and community.

Data Storage Investigations

By the time you read this, TikTok may not be available in the United States and perhaps not in the United Kingdom, either.

In mid-2019, the UK began investigating how TikTok collected and used children's account data. This investigation came on the heels of a U.S. Federal Trade Commission fine of $5.7 million against TikTok in February 2019 for illegally collecting children's personal information.

In 2019, U.S. lawmakers in Congress expressed concerns that TikTok was censoring information, especially videos of the Hong Kong democracy protests, and sending user data to the Chinese government.

These concerns led to a formal national security review by U.S. federal government agencies. The U.S. Army and U.S. Navy have also banned their personnel from using TikTok on government-owned phones because they consider it a security risk.

For its part, ByteDance has pledged to cooperate fully with the U.S. government to assuage its concerns, but that promise was met with deep skepticism by Congress when the company refused to testify before the Senate Judiciary Committee in November 2019.

If you're a current TikTok user or want to be, keep an eye on the news because this saga still may not be resolved by the time you read this.

Now that you know about the ten social networking websites with the biggest demographics, in Chapter 5 we'll home in on five of those websites with the broadest user bases and learn about their formatting requirements for graphics and links. But first let's take a look at exactly how you can use social media and content marketing as a tool to build your business.

Chapter 3

The Roles of Social Media and Content Marketing

So here's how content marketing and social media work. You create a website and a blog. You create branded social profiles for your business on the major social networks. Then each time you publish a new blog post, you push those social sharing buttons at the bottom of the post, and now you're using social media to market your blog, right?

Not so fast.

First let's be clear: Social media is not there to market your blog. In fact, marketing your blog shouldn't be a goal at all. Your marketing should be all about promoting your brand and using your platform to grow and educate your audience. Your blog, therefore, is part of your overall marketing strategy.

We may talk a lot about blog promotion, but by that we mean that you're using the blog, and the blog's content, as a tool to market your business.

This is an important point, because if you approach social media without a blog or content plan, you lose opportunities to leverage many of the benefits social media can offer. While determining your content plan is beyond the scope of this book, you'll find plenty of resources on Mike's Blogging Brute site if needed, and we'll assume you're prepared to create and use website content accordingly.

So the rest of this chapter will focus on how you can use social media and content together as a wonderful tool for building your business. Specifically, we will discuss a number of approaches where social media and content complement and enhance each other.

We'll start with how content can be used to create activity (shares) to your social profiles, which can deliver value and, of course, drive referral traffic. We'll use those shares to build authority and drive conversations. We'll then discuss how content and social media can be leveraged with influencers and other social media angles to achieve your business goals.

SOCIAL SHARING

Of course, the obvious way to market and promote your brand and content is through those initial social shares. But even then, just hitting all the buttons isn't the way to go.

Social media is not a broadcast channel for your business. It's a way for you to connect and engage with your audience, which means you need to share your new content in a way that's sociable and conversational.

On Facebook, Twitter, Pinterest, and LinkedIn, you have an opportunity to introduce your latest post and explain to your audience why they should be interested in reading it. It only takes a few minutes for you to write a sentence or three, and the result will be a dramatic increase in engagement and referral traffic.

Think about it. If you just spam your post to Facebook, you're relying on your post title, and perhaps an image (if you set it up right) to entice your readers. On the other hand, if you talk about why you've written the article, and perhaps ask a direct question, people will be more likely to take an interest. In this way, you'll be delivering value and interest right from the start, which will help to further your relationship.

Otherwise, you're just asking your connections to do you a favor, and you'll soon spend whatever capital you might have earned.

Of course, the obvious question here is, how do you know whether you're seeing a real ROI from your social media activity? Google Analytics, a free website reporting tool you can install from Google, will tell you where your referral traffic is coming from, and if you set up goals on Analytics, like online purchases, sign-ups, or contacts, you can see that, too.

Additionally, the major social platforms offer high-level insights on follower growth and engagement. We will spend a great deal of time discussing metrics and reporting tools in Chapter 13.

But if you want to get a clearer picture across multiple channels, you're going to need a social media management tool like Agorapulse. You'll be able to track over time how your social campaigns are helping to build your brand awareness and authority, and ultimately contributing to sales.

Don't worry, we'll explain more about what Agorapulse is and does later on. For now, just know that there are tools available to you, both free and paid, native and third party, that will help you measure your success.

AUTHORITY BUILDING

Now take a step back for a moment, and think about all the blog posts you share to social media. Are they on topic? If they are, then over time you should develop a reputation as an authority on that topic.

For example, throughout 2013, Mike often blogged about Hootsuite, another social media management tool. He wrote articles on how to use it, as well as updates on the latest changes and features. Over time, he developed a reputation as an expert on Hootsuite, so much so that Hootsuite asked to syndicate nine of his articles on their blog and referred to him as the most knowledgeable person on Hootsuite outside of Hootsuite. Within a year, he'd published a book on how to use Hootsuite. He used the power of social media to build his brand as a Hootsuite authority. You can do the same—build your authority on any number of topics and solidify your ethos as a subject-matter expert.

By constantly sharing those articles about Hootsuite to social media, he gave his budding reputation a jump-start. But that's not where the real authority building took place.

That happened on other people's posts and events.

Again, remember that social media's purpose isn't to promote business or content; it's to form relationships and develop them through conversations and discussions. And today, that exists in two basic forms: comment exchanges and live video discussions.

You can go into Facebook groups, LinkedIn groups, and other social media communities to find other people talking about your industry and relevant topics. You'll note that they're raising points, sharing content of their own, and most important, asking questions.

The most effective thing you can do with your blog content, and to promote your business overall, is to notice someone asking a question that you've already answered in a blog post, and direct them to it. Simply say, "Hey! That's a great question. I went in depth on that topic in this post: (insert link) and I think you'll find all your answers there. Check it out and let me know if you have more questions."

To the person asking the question, that's incredibly powerful. You just simultaneously demonstrated helpfulness and expertise, not to mention accessibility. That person is going to be very grateful and interested in what else you've written. They're a hundred times more likely than a random visitor from Twitter to share your post and subscribe to your email list. (And don't forget your comment on a public post will be seen by others as well!)

Similarly, livestreaming on Facebook, YouTube, LinkedIn, and Periscope offers the opportunity for multiple people to participate in live video discussions on whatever topics they wish. The moment Mike started to appear on other people's video broadcasts and talk to their audiences about how to get more out of Hootsuite was the moment his reputation took off.

And each time, he would provide very specific examples that were derived from blog content he'd already written. In fact, Mike was always thrilled to find that when he'd mention a particular blog post, the show host or even an audience member would go grab the link and share it in the comments for other audience members to check out.

More on how this works in a moment.

Now, let's combine the initial social sharing approach we mentioned earlier and the authority building approach we just talked about, and see how we can spark some conversations of our own.

Those initial shares to your social profiles are great, and in fact, you should be resharing your content to those social profiles on a regular basis (since you're always gaining new fans, and only a small fraction of your total fans would have seen the initial post). But even if you were able to get your blog content in front of all your followers, you'd still be talking about a relatively small number of people.

When you participate in other people's discussions or live video events, that's an opportunity to expand into larger groups of people who have potentially never heard of you. But the limitation there is that you have to wait for someone to post the right question or wait to be invited on someone's show. And those are opportunities that you simply cannot force or predict.

So that means it's up to us to spark some discussions of our own.

Social Groups

The first place to look for discussions to participate in is those same Facebook groups, LinkedIn groups, and other specialized communities. You can also include Twitter chats, Quora, and other online platforms where you're able to start a conversation around a topic.

Just as with the initial social sharing, you have to be clever and respectful when you go about this. These destinations are not simply places to broadcast your links. And in fact, many social groups do not permit links at all. So be mindful of whatever rules and requirements an individual group has in place.

(Note that most groups and communities have a pinned post or group description where the basic rules are laid out. Just remember that for the most part, the group just wants to make sure it's not filled with spammed posts, and that the posts are created for real discussion that benefits the group.)

The idea is simple. Start a new discussion based around the topic you've blogged about. You might ask a question that relates to the post, or, better yet, take a position that is somewhat polarizing and watch how people flock to one side or the other.

For instance, among marketers, one of the most hated Twitter features was the Auto Direct Message (DM). Using any number of available tools, you could set it up so that any time someone new followed you on Twitter, the tool automatically sent them a direct message.

Which of course the spammers completely ruined.

But Mike wrote a blog post about how great the Auto DM could be if used properly, and shared it to a number of social media groups and communities. His introduction was designed to spark those negative feelings toward Auto DMs and get people commenting on the posts.

And it worked like a charm.

There were plenty of people who remarked that they hated Auto DMs and obviously didn't bother to read the article, but there were plenty of others who read the article and came back to the group discussion to share their thoughts on the stance.

We've taken the time to identify and join all kinds of marketing and social media groups and communities on Facebook and LinkedIn so that every time we have a new piece of content, it's just a matter of finding the perfect communities and the perfect angle through which to get a conversation going related to the blog post we want to share.

This brings up a really important point: Don't wait until you have a relevant blog post or promotion to join communities. Start now.

Begin finding and joining communities that you think will be mutually beneficial, and begin participating in the conversations taking place. That way, when you're ready to share something of your own, you're not a complete stranger to the group.

For instance, if your business is focused on a specific geographic region, such as St. Louis, Missouri, take a few minutes to search Facebook and LinkedIn for groups of other professionals there. You might find general groups, like "St. Louis Entrepreneurs," where you will be able to connect with other professionals, as well as industry-specific groups like "STL Digital Marketers."

Live Video

A somewhat similar slant involves the live video events that are going on constantly. At any time, you can see what Facebook, Periscope, or YouTube videos are live and start watching any that are of interest to you.

While the technical formats are different, the basic tenets are the same. One or more people will be participating in a live discussion and broadcasting their video and audio from their computers, while an unlimited number of viewers can be watching the live feed.

Audience members can chat with each other in the comments, mention that they liked something that was just said, or ask questions. Depending on the show format, participants can choose to answer questions live or perhaps come back and address comments after the show (if it's a more formal presentation).

Sometimes there will be questions that the show participants don't have the perfect answer for, and that's where you and your content come in.

As an audience member, you're free to share links to resources if appropriate. Of course, we don't want to just spam links to our own blog posts, so be judicious. And, just as with social groups, make sure that the first comment you make isn't a link to a blog post. You have to participate naturally, which means doing things like saying hi, asking some questions of your own, and so on.

Better yet, if you are a regular attendee to some shows (many people use Facebook Live to broadcast a regularly scheduled show that you can attend week after week), and you add to the show by participating and providing useful information, you may be invited to jump into an open slot during a show or perhaps be a featured guest in the future.

As we mentioned before, that's what happened to Mike with regard to Hootsuite, and it made a tremendous difference in his business and reputation.

Spend some time familiarizing yourself with those platforms, and keep an eye out for others. Facebook Live and others are one-to-many broadcast platforms, so they work a little differently. We'll talk about this quite a bit in Chapter 11.

BROADCAST TEACHING

Yet another way that businesses can leverage social media, and live video in particular, is to teach a live audience about a topic.

On average, when giving a presentation, you'll deliver about 130 words per minute. That means an existing 1,250-word blog post will work out to a perfect ten-minute presentation.

Now, simply reading a blog post on a video platform like Periscope probably wouldn't be very interesting to your audience. But you can hit all the highlights of your post in about three minutes.

And three-minute videos are particularly popular.

The real beauty of videos, whether you're hosting a full-length show or making a quick Periscope broadcast, is that they can be repurposed. You can take a video from Periscope and upload it to YouTube and Facebook. You can pin it to Pinterest.

You can embed it on the original blog post or other blog posts, particularly if there's a short snippet that answers a specific question well. You can pull out the audio and use that for a podcast, further extending your reach into an untapped audience.

Sometimes you might even reverse the process: Start with a video interview, and turn that into a blog post.

INFLUENCER MARKETING

This brings us to influencer marketing—the use of other experts in your industry who already have a sizable audience that respects and trusts them.

Regardless of what industry you're in, there are likely other people in your field who have a more established reputation and audience. Maybe they have larger social followings, are published authors, or are a mainstream media celebrity.

These are people you can learn from, and it would be particularly valuable to have a relationship with them.

Of course, the obvious benefit to you is that when someone like that shares something you've written to their followers, you reach a vastly wider audience. But there are far more glorious and subtler benefits, which we'll discuss in more detail in Chapter 10.

You can't expect that an influencer will share your latest blog post unless you already have a relationship in place—one where they've come to recognize your expertise and look forward to seeing your new content, just like the rest of your readers do.

That said, there are things you can do to help foster relationships with the influencers in your niche. Then you should just wait to see what develops. If you have a set agenda, or want things to happen on your timetable, you're going to be disappointed and come off as disingenuous.

Social media can be a great equalizer, particularly on Twitter and Instagram, where you can follow anyone you want. Simply find the influencers in your niche, follow them, and begin to engage with them naturally. You know—like a real human being who isn't a stalker.

Reply or comment on posts that interest you, and share posts you think your own audience would be interested in. If the influencer is blogging, become an active reader and engage with them on their blog with insightful comments and questions.

That will get you on their radar.

The next step is to begin to include them in your own content: by quoting them, linking to their blog posts, or including them in *roundups*, where you ask their opinion on a topic and publish opinions from a group of influencers.

Or you could do a live video interview (you read about that earlier in the chapter). Instead of being on someone else's video, broadcast your own, and invite a key influencer to be your guest. It's more work on your part to organize and promote, to be sure, but it's also a tremendous opportunity for content creation.

You can center the show on a blog post you've already written, creating more interest in that post, or pick an entirely new topic and turn the recorded video into a follow-up post. Either way, the influencer who's involved will likely help share the event and materials.

We've done many such shows with guests like Guy Kawasaki and *Pretty Woman* producer Gary W. Goldstein, and they've all been tremendously successful on a number of levels.

Chapter 10 goes into more detail on influencer marketing, including how to identify and work with key influencers in your niche.

DARK SOCIAL MEDIA

The one area you can't measure is *dark social media*. This refers to all the ways people can share your content with other people without your knowledge. Examples include emails, text messages, and direct social messages. In each of these cases, someone decided to share your content with one or more people, but they did so in a way that couldn't be accurately measured or recorded.

While it's unfortunate that you're unable to track the impact of dark social media, that doesn't mean you should ignore it. In fact, you should make it as easy as possible for people to share your work this way if they want to.

For instance, consider putting email buttons on all your blog posts. Or, better yet, just make sure that your social sharing buttons include an Other button that links to email, texting apps like WhatsApp, and whatever other choices someone might want to take advantage of.

Within your email newsletters, include social sharing buttons and an invitation to share the newsletter via email along with a note that says, "Did someone email you this newsletter? Make sure you don't miss another by subscribing yourself."

And, of course, make sure all your blog posts have a strong call to action to either read another post, head over to a landing page, or at least sign up for your email list so that you can further capture some of those dark social readers.

PAID SOCIAL MEDIA

Finally, you should strongly consider incorporating paid social media in your marketing strategy. Every social platform now offers the ability to "promote" posts, allowing them to be seen by far more people than your existing follower base.

But be careful. It's easy to run up costs without seeing a real ROI. Make sure that you're using the best platform for your business, targeting the right audience, and sending that targeted traffic to the best possible content.

So let's bring this back to your latest piece of content. Think about who you're targeting with it. Is there a particular network where they're more likely to be active?

Frankly, one of the least expensive platforms to advertise on is Facebook. It also has the best targeting and sports the largest global user base. So that's probably a good place to start. But do give Twitter, LinkedIn, Pinterest, and Instagram due consideration. Chapter 9 will help you distinguish among advertising on the different networks, their content, and their audiences.

We find that the best content to promote on Facebook is content that's particularly strong for driving email sign-ups. Perhaps it has a content upgrade or related ebook that readers can download for free, creating targeted leads for your business.

A nice Facebook campaign, for just a few bucks a day, can send hundreds of readers and prospects to your blog post and business. So give that a try. Chapter 9 will show you how.

AT THE END OF THE DAY

We know we've covered a lot of ground in this chapter—that was deliberate. We wanted to make sure you had a complete picture of how social media can be used to market your business and coordinate with your content. But we don't expect you to tackle all these techniques tomorrow.

Instead, start with social sharing, and take the time to get that right. Then move on to authority building, and so on. As you progress through the various strategies we talked about in this chapter, you'll find that it naturally follows your progression as a business marketer overall.

If you've just published your first blog post, you can't just skip down to influencer marketing. You have to have a consistent history of delivering quality content to establish the credibility you need to form relationships with influencers in your field.

The rest of this book will take a closer look at all these concepts so that you're armed with all the knowledge and foresight you need to be successful. We'll start with the fundamentals: creating your social media strategy.

Chapter 4

Craft Your
Social Media Strategy

This might actually be the single most important chapter of this book. Not only are we going to cover concepts that tie together virtually every other topic in this tome, but just the fact that you're interested in coming up with a social media strategy to begin with is of paramount importance.

You see, that's actually where most businesses (including your competition) fail.

According to Statista, as of 2019, more than 90 percent of businesses in the U.S. used social media for marketing. That's great, because billions of potential customers actively use social networking sites every day. But astoundingly, only "28 percent of marketers have either already implemented social commerce or plan to do so in the next year," according to a 2019 survey by Hootsuite, and only 34 percent measure social ROI.

While a marketer might find those numbers somewhat depressing, as a business owner, you should be elated! Why? Because it's very likely that by simply creating a social media strategy, looking for ways to implement social commerce, and measuring the results, you'll be ahead of your competitors.

Imagine for a moment that you and one other business are the only solution providers in your industry. A prospective customer begins to research their options and discovers both businesses. Your business has an active Twitter presence and creates valuable live video content every week that showcases industry knowledge and invites viewers to free demonstrations. Your competitor posts motivational quotes once in a while.

Everything else being equal, which business would you choose if you were the prospect?

Having that kind of social media presence, and a plan to implement it, is what we're going to cover in this chapter. We're going to determine your strengths and assets, create some goals, and then pull all that together into a viable social media marketing plan.

DETERMINE YOUR STRENGTHS

This section might more aptly be called "Determine Your SWOT." If you're not familiar with SWOT analysis, it stands for "strengths, weaknesses, opportunities, and threats," and it's a way for you and your business to self-assess.

While typically applied to your overall business, industry, and positioning, you should do a SWOT analysis specifically for social media and, if you wish, your overall online marketing plan (which includes your website, blog, and any other content marketing you do online).

You'll find strengths and weaknesses internal to your business, such as having someone available (or not) to manage social channels, writing experience, comfort level on camera, and so on. You'll also find opportunities and threats external to your business, which might include influencers in love with your brand or competitors that dominate the market.

Take the time to consider and write down all your brand's strengths, weaknesses, opportunities, and threats. If you have a team, give them a chance to weigh in. If you're a solopreneur, this would be a great time to form a mastermind group or board of advisers for yourself—some outside folks who will speak truth to you (more on that later).

To help you get started, we're going to give you some strengths and opportunities to consider (see Figure 4–1, on page 45).

After you've identified your strengths, as well as the other elements of the SWOT analysis, you'll better understand what will be easy for you to tackle, or what may present a challenge for you; where you should allot your time and resources, and where you might need to get additional help.

But before we get into that, there are a few more determinations you should make.

DETERMINE YOUR ASSETS

While some SWOT exercises may include assets as strengths, we like to break them out separately when it comes to online marketing and consider things like profiles, apps, and equipment. Obviously having an existing Facebook Page fan base of 100,000 would be considered an asset. But already owning a DSLR camera you can use for photography or live streaming video is also an asset.

Strengths and Opportunities

Strengths

- 2+ hours per week available to spend on marketing _____
  _____

- Experience/skill writing or editing _____
  _____

- Experience/skill creating graphics _____
  _____

- Experience/skill creating video _____
  _____

- Existing brand style guide _____
  _____

- Existing brand values documented _____
  _____

Opportunities

- Few competing brands active on social media _____
  _____

- Little/poor relevant video content _____
  _____

- Brand/industry that favors visuals (e.g., food) _____
  _____

- Wide range of available influencers _____
  _____

- Brand solves a commonly discussed pain point _____
  _____

- Few existing communities within industry/customers _____
  _____

FIGURE 4–1. Strengths and Opportunities Worksheet

As you work through the rest of this chapter (and this book), you must take what we teach you and apply it to your own business, industry, and target audience. Sometimes we will present you with a choice, such as posting images or video, and you will have to decide which is better for your brand.

That is where it will help to have thought about your strengths and assets. If you know you're comfortable on camera and already own a good video camera, the decision to go with video becomes an easier one.

Take a moment to consider all the assets you currently have at your disposal. We've come up with a few ideas to get you started:

1. Existing social channels/audience
2. Existing graphic design software (e.g., Adobe Photoshop)
3. Existing audio/video equipment (e.g., webcam, DSLR)
4. Existing library of media
5. Existing website/email subscribers
6. Available budget

While considering your assets, you might also think of additional strengths, weaknesses, opportunities, or threats. Update those lists as you go.

For instance, while you might consider a large Twitter following an asset, you may also realize that not having any presence on YouTube, Pinterest, or Instagram is a weakness, which should be noted as such.

DETERMINE YOUR GOALS

Start by identifying what your business goals are. Think about the nature of your business and what would make it a success, and follow the reverse of our digital marketing funnel. Are you looking for sales or referrals? Leads? Traffic? Brand mentions? Social followers?

Note and prioritize each goal.

Now think about some specific performance levels and how quickly you want to reach them. How many sales do you want to target? How many leads will you need to be able to convert that many sales? How much traffic will you need to generate that many leads?

You could use specific values here, like units or dollars, or you could employ percentage increases month over month or year over year. Or you could use all of the above. It depends on your business model and how you choose to measure your goals.

A good rule of thumb is to use the "one percent" rule: One percent of your traffic will convert to leads, and one percent of those leads will convert to sales. Over time, through testing and experimentation (and depending on your industry), you'll rise above that level. But for planning purposes, it's an acceptable place to start. It may seem daunting to think you need 1,000 visitors for just one sale, but we'd rather be pleasantly surprised because we overestimated than find ourselves disappointed and unprepared because we underestimated.

When it comes to social media, rather than place emphasis on specific follower counts or social signals, the preferred methodology is to watch for increasing trends. You want to gain followers each week and get more likes and shares, day after day. To that end, watch what you try on social media and pay attention to which techniques yield the most fruit.

By now you should have some notes that look something like this:

1. Sales—10 within first 30 days
2. Leads/email subscribers—1,000 within first 30 days
3. Traffic—10,000+ within first 30 days
4. Increasing brand mentions on social media
5. Increasing followers on social media

Of course, every business is different. Inexpensive products that target regular consumers are easier to sell than expensive B2B services. But you'll likely need less traffic and fewer leads to achieve profitability with a high-end offering. And remember that paid marketing and advertising can put you in front of targeted leads much faster than what you'd achieve organically.

The less money you have to invest in marketing, the lower your expectations may have to be.

DETERMINE YOUR PLAN

While we started by saying that having a strategy is critical, we should probably amend that to say that "having a plan is critical." And to create a successful plan, we should take a moment to review how all these pieces can work together to achieve results for your business. (We will include website content so you have the full picture of how social media works in tandem with the rest of your marketing.)

You may have heard of sales funnels in the past. Digital marketing works along the same lines. Here's a typical sales funnel:

Awareness

↓

Opinion

↓

Consideration

↓

Preference

↓

Purchase

Imagine the bottom of the funnel, the narrowest part or mouth: This is the point where your prospects decide to become customers. It might be an online purchase from your website, a clickthrough to an affiliate site, or a phone call to place an order. The details, of course, will vary depending on your business. This is what is known as the *conversion point* of the process.

As you move up the funnel, it widens to include pages within your site that educate the prospect on who you are, how you can solve their problems, and the specific products or services you offer. These are commonly referred to as landing pages, which are the *consideration point* of the process—when prospects are comparing you and your services with available alternatives.

Above that, the digital marketing funnel typically includes blog posts and other content within your site that visitors may read and later come back to. In this *discovery point*, prospects may be educating themselves about their problems as well as about you.

At the top of the digital marketing funnel, we have what we call "outposts." These are social media profiles and channels, guest blog posts, search engine listings, email, referrals, and so on. Through these mediums, prospects are at the *exposure point*, where they may be hearing about you and your services for the first time, or perhaps they're looking for information on a topic that you've addressed.

It's important to note that, unlike the traditional sales funnel, the digital marketing funnel continues beyond conversion. Since prospects who have become customers will continue to visit your website, read your blog posts, and subscribe to your emails, your marketing efforts contribute to ongoing customer relationships and retention, both of which are critical components of a sustainable business.

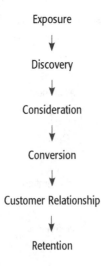

Exposure

↓

Discovery

↓

Consideration

↓

Conversion

↓

Customer Relationship

↓

Retention

With those concepts in mind, and the collection of strengths, assets, and business goals you identified earlier, you can start to assemble your overall plan for a successful social media presence that delivers real ROI.

Earlier chapters set the stage for social media marketing by outlining today's networks and important concepts. The rest of our chapters will give you deep dives into specific tactics and approaches, including live video, chatbots, influencer marketing, and more. As you read through the remaining pages, continue to consider your marketing plan and how each new tactic might complement or enhance what you've already planned to do.

At a higher level, your marketing approach will be to create interesting and helpful content that educates readers on the subject, presents you as an authority, and puts them in a position to hire you or buy from you.

Of course, not every post and activity should be directly focused on generating sales. When it comes to social media, you definitely do not want to be too pushy with your messaging. Instead, recall that the top of the funnel is about exposure. Creating social media activity that generates dialogue is far more effective. Try to balance business content with consumer-focused content (articles, fun facts, behind the scenes, etc.) that will appeal to your target audience organically yet remains in line with your business model and industry.

That starts with creating content on property you own yourself: your website.

Content Schedule

First, decide how often you're going to add new content to your website. Whether it's in the form of pages or blog posts is up to you. But you need a publishing schedule, and initially it needs to be inviolable. If you allow yourself to stray from this schedule early on, it will be too hard to get back on track, and before you know it, you're way behind in your marketing.

Now, for a startup business and website, it's important to get rolling as quickly as you can, and that means a high rate of publication at first. Generally, we recommend at least three to five pages or blog posts per week for the first six months. After that, if things are going well, you can ratchet down to two to three per week, and then eventually down to one per week/month.

A few years ago, marketing platform HubSpot analyzed some business blogs and their relative search engine traffic and lead generation. On average, most business blogs began to see an exponential increase in search engine referral traffic after they'd published more than 50 pieces of content. Lead generation rose accordingly.

That means that typically, if you post just once per week, it will be a year before you begin to see real gains in referral traffic.

Note that if writing isn't your jam, you can absolutely create video or even audio content instead. However, you will still need to embed that media onto your site and surround it with text to give Google and your readers context. You might also consider starting with video and repurposing it into written content, which we'll cover extensively in Chapter 11.

Content Topics

Next, think about what you're going to write or talk about. Again, this is going to be a combination of landing pages and blog posts (or videos, podcasts, etc.).

Your landing pages should focus on the areas in which you are establishing yourself as an expert. For each main landing page, consider two to three topics on which you could write and add as subpages. And then, for each of those subpages, think about two to three blog posts you can write relating to those topics.

When you're through, you will have all your site's most important content mapped out. You don't have to write it all overnight, and you can certainly mix other blog posts into your publishing schedule as topics come to mind. But now you have a plan.

One of the great uses of keyword research tools is to brainstorm content topics. You can actually see the phrases (keywords) that people are searching on and use those to develop ideas for new pages or posts.

Try to tell stories as you write. Whether on your landing pages or in blog posts, stories bring your audience into the room with you, while you weave in details of your expertise.

Social Media Prioritization

Next, think about the social networks you're going to be active on. There's no "right" answer here. Rather, there are a number of things to consider, such as:

- Which social networks are you already active on?
- Which social networks have an audience that seems best suited to your business?
- Which social networks favor the type of content you prefer or are able to create?
- Do you have a personal preference?

While considering those points, let's put the major social networks into tiers. While we think you should create a professional profile on every social network, you only need to maintain constant activity on one or two platforms. Like this:

- Tier One: Facebook, Twitter
- Tier Two: LinkedIn, Pinterest, Instagram
- Tier Three: Periscope, Google My Business, YouTube, SlideShare, etc.

For Facebook, Twitter, Pinterest, LinkedIn, and YouTube, you will need a "cover photo": a custom graphic branded to reflect your business (and tie into your overall marketing image). And for all social profiles, use a professional logo or professional-looking head shot for the profile image. If you don't have the budget for a graphic designer, check out the website Canva. (We'll talk more about image creation and each network's requirements in Chapters 5 and 6.)

Social Media Activity

Instructions on how to use each social network is outside our scope, as it would require a book in itself to outline techniques and best practices for even just the top five or six networks.

Here are the basics you need to keep in mind and integrate into your marketing plan.

1. Remember that social media is not an advertising medium. It's an opportunity for you to connect with prospects, readers, and potential partners. It's a place where you can share content and information, offer value and assistance, and create a reputation.

   Don't blow it.

   If you always think about how or whether a particular post will be interesting and helpful to your audience, you'll make good progress.

2. Every time you publish a new piece of content to your website, share it to social media. Once you've selected your top-priority network, research best practices for sharing to that network so that your shares look and perform optimally.

   Every social network has its own unique set of best practices, so be mindful of them. For instance, you might share new blog posts to Facebook or Instagram only once, but consider tweeting about them three to four times the first day, once or twice the second day, and then have them in a rotation to be routinely tweeted along with your other content. LinkedIn and Pinterest audiences may tolerate a second share later in the day, but no more.

   Any frequency you choose to adopt must be tempered by the size of your audience, the platform, and your posting history. If, for instance, yours is a new Twitter profile, talking about the same blog post four times in a day would be too much. This is very much a case of using your best judgment!

3. When you're not sharing new blog content, share content and articles from other sources that will also be helpful and interesting to your audience. This is called *curated content*. The easiest way to do this is to identify several sources of information that regularly publish new posts and aren't direct competitors. You can then subscribe to their RSS feeds using Feedly. The RSS feed

just shares new content, and a reader like Feedly allows you to see it (and even share it).

4. Find other experts in your field and industry who are active on social media, regularly providing value, and with whom you would be interested in forming a stronger relationship. These people are "influencers" and represent a powerful marketing opportunity. If an influencer in your niche decides to share one of your blog posts, you might see more traffic in a day than you did all last month. So pick a few, begin following them, and regularly reshare some of their helpful material. (Chapter 10 will cover this extensively.)

5. Prepare a series of business-related messages that you can use to remind your audience who you are and what you do. These will only be shared sparingly—perhaps once a week or month. But make sure you're including them. It might be a sales message, an invitation to subscribe to your newsletter, or just a link to follow you on your primary network.

You can now set a social media activity schedule that looks something like this:

- *Facebook*: New blog post share, 1 curated content share
- *Twitter*: New blog post share, 4 curated content shares, 2 influencers retweets, 2 archived posts
- *LinkedIn*: New blog post share, 1 curated content share

Modify as needed to reflect your own network priorities and desired levels of activity.

Use a social media management tool like Agorapulse to schedule much of this activity in advance, leaving you free to focus on your day-to-day business needs. However, you will want to spend a little time each day on your most important social network connecting with others, commenting on posts, and simply engaging with people.

Also be sure to keep an eye out for comments and mentions from your followers and always respond and thank people in a timely fashion. How fast is necessary depends on your business and audience. A small retail shop can likely check in once or twice a day, while a business that consumers are relying on may need to make sure every hour is covered.

Airlines, for instance, must keep on top of their social channels for customer service reasons. Customers are turning to social media to be heard, and it's critical that you respond within a reasonable amount of time.

Search Engine Optimization

While SEO as a topic is outside the scope of this book, great SEO can actually help your social media presence. More organic traffic to your site and content will raise brand awareness, create more opportunities to grow your social following and community, and generate more organic shares of your content to new audiences.

So let's quickly go over some basics.

When it comes to SEO, as we mentioned before, one of the best things you can do is research your topics ahead of time using a keyword research tool, and then create content for those topics. We recommend a tool called SEMrush.

Beyond that, here are some general tips to keep in mind as you go:

- Register your site with a free Google Search Console account to monitor your site, see how many pages have been indexed, and submit a sitemap.
- Use your targeted keywords as often as possible while still sounding natural. Do not "stuff" them by using them excessively.
- Use lots of images, and use keywords in image filenames and alt tags. Not only does this help with search, content with more images is more likely to be read entirely and therefore shared more often.
- Don't worry about the keywords meta tag, but do fill in all other meta tags appropriately.
- Use SEMrush to routinely audit your site and note errors and issues that you may need to address.

Social Media and/or Search Engine Paid Advertising

We're going to devote an entire chapter to paid advertising (Chapter 9), so we don't need to go into detail here on techniques. But for planning purposes, it's important to create a budget for paid advertising and understand how it can be used to support your plan and business goals.

All the major social networks offer paid advertising options to reach new audiences and promote your brand. You can also take advantage of search intent and put your problem-solving content and landing pages in front of search audiences when they're using Google or Bing to find answers.

Must you advertise to succeed on social media? Not necessarily. A lot will depend on your industry and what the competition is like, as well as your business goals and timeframe for achieving them. Generally you'll find that paid advertising is most successful when it's used to amplify great organic marketing activities.

In other words, study the rest of this book closely to learn exactly what kinds of social media activities will work best for you and your audience, do those, and then consider putting some money behind promoting and helping to spread that great activity.

Remember that your marketing plan is a dynamic and living document, designed to change and adapt and grow right alongside your business. If you decide to focus on, say, Facebook initially, that doesn't mean you can't shift to Instagram after six months. Figure 4–2 shows you a simple template for a basic marketing plan. Feel free to tweak it to fit your needs.

Marketing Plan Worksheet

My Business Goals

1. _____
2. _____
3. _____
4. _____
5. _____

My Business Assets

Total Budget: _____

Total Staff: _____

Website: _____

Social Profiles: _____

Materials: _____

Content

Publishing Schedule: _____

Landing Page: _____

Subpages: _____

Blog Post Topics: _____

Social Networks

Tier 1: _____

Tier 2: _____

Tier 3: _____

Sources: _____

Influencers: _____

FIGURE 4–2. Marketing Plan Worksheet

Marketing Plan Worksheet

Activity

Network: _____   Frequency: _____

Network: _____   Frequency: _____

Network: _____   Frequency: _____

Network: _____   Frequency: _____

Network: _____   Frequency: _____

Targeted Keywords:

1. _____

2. _____

3. _____

Google Ads Budget: _____

Facebook Budget: _____

Other Ad Budget: _____

Tool: _____   Cost: _____

Tool: _____   Cost: _____

Tool: _____   Cost: _____

Tool: _____   Cost: _____

Tool: _____   Cost: _____

FIGURE 4–2. Marketing Plan Worksheet, continued

This is where the measurement and learning comes in. If you treat every marketing strategy and technique as an experiment and open yourself to listening to the data, you will be able to make sound business decisions and smart changes in direction.

Chapter 5

Understand Today's Format Types

Social networking websites are a lot like anything else computer-related: They make our lives richer, more interesting . . . and more complicated. That's why you're reading this old-fashioned thing called a book. This chapter will tell you everything you need to know about the websites' different format types and specifications, so you can keep your profiles and posts as current as possible.

Each social networking website has its own format requirements, so to keep this chapter at a manageable size, we've focused on the five social networks with the broadest user bases:

1. Facebook
2. LinkedIn
3. Twitter
4. YouTube
5. Instagram

Social networking websites are always changing, but the specifications in this chapter will give you a good idea of what to expect. The information in this chapter is current as of early 2020, but you should always search the help section on the social network's website for graphic and/or video requirements to ensure there haven't been any recent changes.

We'll start by giving you the dimensions you need for graphics like your profile photos, as well as for banners that social networks like you to use in your profiles. Next, we'll talk about required image sizes within a post. Then we'll talk about the technical requirements for posting videos—including on YouTube, of course. Finally, we'll discuss website link formatting requirements.

GRAPHIC REQUIREMENTS

Graphics on your social networking profiles include the *cover photo*, which is a large, banner-sized photo at the top of your personal, company, or group profile, as well as your *profile photo*, a smaller, thumbnail-sized photo that people can see on your homepage and that appears with your comments on other pages. The following requirements were taken directly from the social networking websites' help pages, and we tested them to ensure they worked.

> **TIP**
>
> Read the community guidelines for the site if you're not sure whether the photos or artwork you plan to upload will pass muster.

Your personal profile photo may be a head shot of yourself. If you have a company profile, such as for your company page on LinkedIn, then you may want to use your company's logo instead. Either way, the technical guidelines are the same, as you'll read about in this section.

Cover Photos

Cover photos are a standard feature on any personal, business, or group profile webpage on a social networking website. For example, Figure 5–1 on page 59 shows the cover photo for the 360 Marketing Squad's group page on Facebook.

One common mistake is to hire a graphic designer who isn't familiar with social networking's requirements to create one cover photo to use with multiple websites. You'll quickly discover that you hit the error trifecta: The graphic that fits on one website doesn't fit on all the others, your company looks unprofessional, and you wasted money instead of saving it.

There are three ways to avoid this memorable experience:

1. As you may have guessed, you can read this book and create the cover photo your-self, with the proper design for each website.
2. Find a designer who knows the cover photo rules for each social media website.
3. Give this book to (or buy another copy for) your graphic designer and put a book-mark or flag on the first page of this chapter.

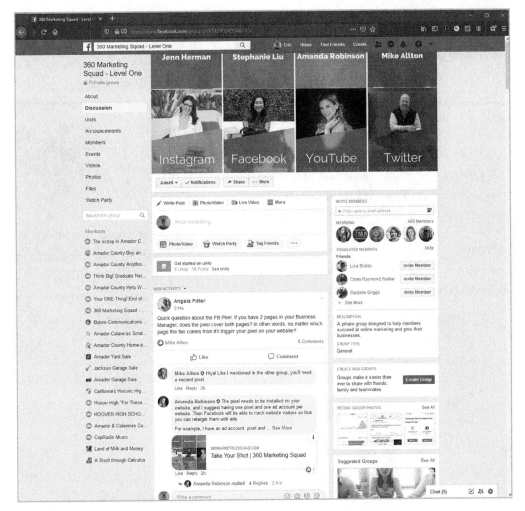

FIGURE 5–1. A typical Facebook cover photo

With options 2 or 3, you'll probably have to pay the graphic designer more money to design each version of the cover photo, but we don't make the rules—we just tell you what they are.

If you choose to handle designing your cover photo yourself, remember to do a quick search on the social networking websites' help centers to get their latest specifications and requirements.

Facebook

Facebook requires that your cover photo be 400 pixels wide by 150 pixels high. However, the site automatically resizes your cover photo to be 820 pixels wide by 312 pixels high on a desktop or laptop (or landscape tablet). On a smartphone, Facebook resizes the photo to 640 pixels wide and 360 pixels high.

The best and least stressful thing to do is take Facebook's advice for creating a cover photo that loads the fastest on their website and mobile site: create an sRGB (short for standard Red Green Blue) graphic in JPEG format that's 851 pixels wide and 315 pixels high. After you create the cover photo with those dimensions and colors, ensure the file is less than 100KB before you upload it to Facebook.

LinkedIn

LinkedIn is much more straightforward when it comes to creating a cover photo:

- The minimum size is 1192 pixels wide by 220 pixels high.
- The preferred size, if you have a video driver and monitor with at least 1920-by-1200 pixel resolution, is 1536 pixels high by 768 pixels wide.
- LinkedIn accepts graphics in PNG, JPEG, and GIF formats.

Twitter

Twitter is also straightforward about its requirements for a cover photo, which Twitter calls a header image. If you have a lower-resolution monitor, you may want to resize the graphic to a smaller size that Twitter can then enlarge while keeping the photo's correct aspect ratio, which is the proportional relationship between its width and height.

Twitter accepts cover photos in JPEG, PNG, and GIF formats. It also prefers a photo that's 1500 pixels wide and 500 pixels high. However, if you can't size a photo to those dimensions, and you're the one designing the cover photo, here's what you need to do:

1. Use a browser size information website such as resizeMyBrowser so you can see how wide your browser window is.
2. Create a new graphic file that's 1500 pixels wide and 500 pixels high in your favorite graphics application. We'll use Adobe Photoshop for this example. (Don't worry about the fact that your cover photo doesn't fit entirely within the Adobe Photoshop window.)
3. Change the image size and enter the width of your browser window. The height changes automatically if the Aspect Ratio icon is selected, as it is by default in

TIP

Even when your cover photo meets the recommended dimensions, always check it on a smartphone, desktop, laptop, and tablet (in landscape orientation). If you see that you have to change the photo to make it look reasonably good on all those devices, take heart: You're learning the little tricks that will make your life easier when you create more cover photos for yourself—or charge more to create them for others.

Adobe Photoshop. Now you can create and upload your cover photo to Twitter.

YouTube

YouTube not only displays its cover photos, which it calls channel art, on desktop and mobile computer screens but also on TV screens. Because these screens are so different and larger cover photos can be cropped, Google recommends that you upload a photo that's 2560 pixels wide by 1440 pixels high and no larger than 6MB.

If your computer's video resolution isn't that high, you may have to put up with seeing only parts

> **TIP** ⓘ
>
> If you upload a photo that isn't 1500 pixels wide by 500 pixels high, Twitter automatically shows the area of your photo that will be shown in your profile. You can move this area around in your photo to choose the part you want people to see.

of the photo at one time and/or shrinking the photo in your favorite graphics program to fit on your screen. You can also design your cover photo to Google's minimum dimensions: 1546 pixels wide by 423 pixels high.

After you upload a cover photo with these dimensions, YouTube centers the photo within the photo area, and it will now appear on any computer, smartphone, or TV browser. What's more, you won't have to shrink the photo (or use the scrollbars as much) to edit it.

Instagram

Instagram doesn't provide a space for cover photos, so you don't need to worry about this size here!

Profile Photos

A profile photo is the photo that appears in the circle on your profile page on all the social networking websites we discuss in this chapter. You can upload any photo you want as long as the photo meets the site's guidelines. If your profile is for your company, you may decide to use your company logo. For your personal profile, you can upload a photo of yourself like the one on Eric's LinkedIn profile, shown in Figure 5–2 on page 62.

The rules for profile photos are far less strict than for cover photos because a profile photo takes up much less space. You still need to follow some rules, though, to make your profile photo look its best. Checking the help centers' entries on "profile photos" will give you the most up-to-date information.

Facebook

In Facebook, size your profile photo to 170 pixels square—that is, 170 pixels wide by 170 pixels high—to display on computers, laptops, and the Facebook app or website on a

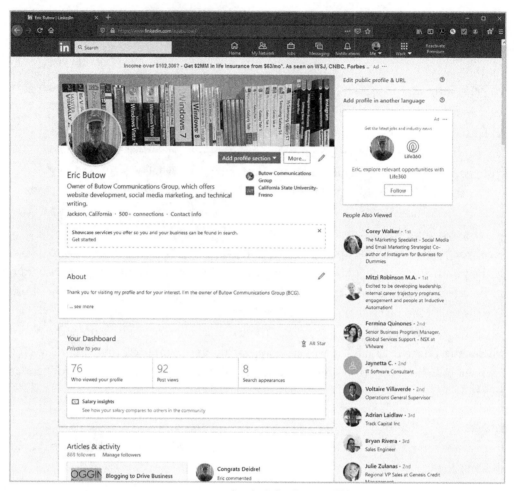

FIGURE 5-2. A standard LinkedIn profile photo

tablet. Facebook will automatically reduce your profile photo to 128 pixels square so it appears properly on a smartphone.

LinkedIn

LinkedIn has the same profile photo requirements for your profile or your company page: The photo must be 300 pixels wide by 300 pixels wide, and LinkedIn accepts photo files in PNG, JPEG, or GIF format.

Twitter

Twitter recommends that your profile photo is 400 pixels wide by 400 pixels high. If it's not, Twitter resizes the photo to fit, and you may not like the results. The site also requires that the profile photo be no larger than 2MB. You can upload the photo in JPEG, GIF, or PNG file format.

YouTube

YouTube uses the profile picture from your Google account, and you can manage your account by clicking on the profile picture (or the placeholder graphic), which YouTube calls the channel icon, in the upper-right corner of the YouTube web page and then clicking Manage Your Google Account in the drop-down menu. The Google Account website appears in a separate browser tab, and you can change the profile picture photo by clicking either on the photo or the placeholder graphic at the top of the web page.

Google recommends that you upload a photo that is 800 pixels wide by 800 pixels high; it accepts BMP, GIF, JPEG, or PNG format. After you upload the photo, Google shrinks it to 98 pixels wide by 98 pixels high so it fits within the photo circle on all Google websites, including YouTube. You can also size your photo to 98 pixels square if you want.

When you're finished, you can close the Google Account tab. The new profile photo may take a few minutes to appear on the YouTube website.

Instagram

The Instagram profile photo is vital to your account, as this is the photo that will define you when you perform any interactions on the website. When you like, comment, post, or otherwise engage with others on Instagram, your profile photo is tied to those interactions.

The minimum size for a profile photo on Instagram is 110 pixels wide by 110 pixels high. The ideal size is closer to around 180 pixels square, though. Be aware that Instagram will crop your profile photo to a circle, so you don't want anything important to appear in the corners.

To edit your profile photo on Instagram, go to your profile on your mobile device (the person icon in the bottom navigation bar) and tap Edit Profile. In the Edit screen, tap the Change Profile Photo option under your photo to upload a new image. You can upload an image from your mobile device or import a photo from Facebook. When you're finished, save your changes by tapping on the check mark in the top right corner of the Edit screen.

PHOTOS IN YOUR POSTS

After you set up your cover and profile photos, you can post to your heart's content. We're confident that like most people, you want to share photos in

> **TIP**
>
> Though we talk about You-Tube in this chapter, it doesn't let you post photos on your feeds—because it's designed for sharing videos, of course. You can still post cover and profile photos, as discussed in the "Graphic Requirements" section earlier in this chapter.

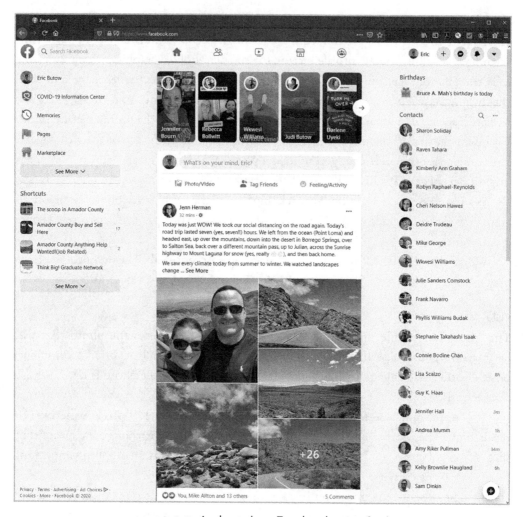

FIGURE 5–3. A photo in a Facebook newsfeed

your posts, such as the ones you see in Figure 5–3. Before you get too carried away, take a deep breath and read through this section so you can make sure that the photos you post in your feeds look good to the people who see them. As always, be sure to consult the individual sites' help sections for the latest updates.

Facebook

When you post an image, it'll show up in the newsfeeds of your followers and friends. If your settings allow everyone on Facebook to view your profile, then your photo may find its way into any Facebook user's newsfeed. Facebook accepts photos in BMP, GIF, JPEG, PNG, or TIFF format.

Consider resizing and/or cropping your photo per Facebook's specifications: 1200 pixels wide by 630 pixels high. When the photo appears in your newsfeed, Facebook automatically resizes it to a maximum width of 470 pixels and changes the height based on the aspect ratio. If you post the photo to a feed on a page (such as one for your company), Facebook uses a width of 504 pixels.

LinkedIn

You can upload photos to your LinkedIn post in GIF, JPEG, or PNG format. LinkedIn recommends that your photo should be 1104 pixels wide by 736 pixels high. This size ensures that LinkedIn can shrink the size of the photo to its standard post dimensions 552 pixels wide by 289 pixels high without any loss in resolution.

However, on a mobile device your image will be cropped at the top or bottom, so check how your photo looks on the LinkedIn app on your mobile phone. Unfortunately, you can't edit the photo after you've posted it, so if it doesn't look the way you want on the app, you'll have to delete the post, tweak your photo, and then try posting it again and hope it will look the way you want this time.

Twitter

Twitter allows you to attach up to four photos to a tweet. If you're uploading one or more photos from your smartphone camera roll to the Twitter app, you can even edit the image within the app. Twitter accepts photos in GIF, JPEG, or PNG format.

Here's what you need to know when you upload a photo:

- The photo needs to be 1024 pixels wide by 512 pixels high.
- The maximum file size for photos is 5MB.
- You can also upload animated GIF files, but the file size varies between mobile and desktop web browsers. The mobile app only accepts animated GIF files smaller than 5MB, but on the Twitter website you can upload an animated GIF smaller than 15MB.

Twitter may shrink your photo to fit depending on how the user's feed is set up. In that case, it shrinks the photo to 506 pixels wide by 253 pixels high. So you need to make sure that the part of the photo you want people to see most is centered in the picture.

Instagram

Instagram allows you to upload photos and videos to your posts. In addition to basic single-image or single-video posts, you can create a carousel post, which can include up to ten photos and/or videos. And for Instagram Stories, you can create photos, videos, or posts with a colored background palette—but remember, they'll disappear after 24 hours.

For feed post sizing, it's ideal to format images and videos as squares. This is how Instagram was designed, and it's still true today. That said, you can upload portrait or landscape posts, too. In terms of ratios for non-square posts, vertical (or portrait) posts should be 4:5. If your image is taller than that, Instagram will crop it to fit that format. For horizontal (or landscape) posts, you can go to a 16:9 ratio, but the wider the image, the less height you have and the less screen coverage you get. So it's best to stay as close to a square as possible.

Now think about the size of those images in terms of pixels. An ideal Instagram image is 1080 pixels square—that is, 1080 pixels wide by 1080 pixels high. The minimum size Instagram will support is 320 pixels square. If your image is smaller than that, Instagram will enlarge it to fit, which may result in pixilation or a blurry photo. And if your image is larger than 1080 pixels square, Instagram will shrink it down—but that won't cause any distortion in your image quality.

For Instagram Stories, photos are formatted in a vertical orientation, traditionally in a 9:16 format. The pixel sizing is similar to feed posts, with 1080 pixels being ideal, so for a Story post, your image should be 1080 pixels wide by 1920 pixels high.

SOCIAL NETWORK ICON RULES

Sometimes you want to show your social savvy on your own website or other marketing efforts by posting icons from all the social platforms you frequent. If you're going to use social media icons, you need to know how to display them properly on your website and in print. Only go to the approved brand websites. (Don't think social media companies aren't keeping an eye out for infractions, either.) Figure 5–4 on page 67 shows how social networking icons should look on a website.

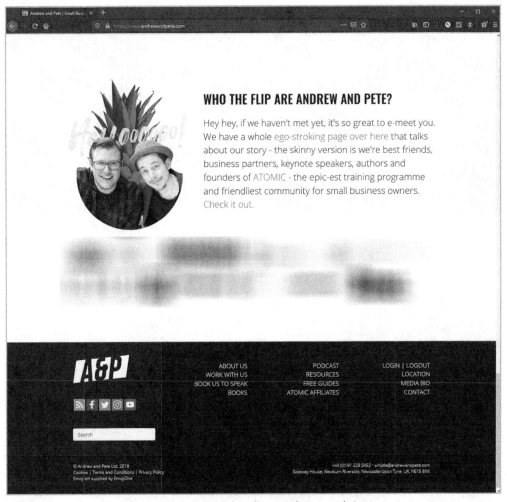

FIGURE 5–4. Typical web social network icons

Facebook

You can get the icon rules for all Facebook's social networking websites (Facebook, Instagram, WhatsApp, etc.) from Facebook's Brand Resource Center. Click on the Facebook App button to open the Facebook App Brand Resources web page, shown in Figure 5–5 on page 68.

Here, you'll find the following information about what you can and can't do with Facebook icons:

■ You can download three icons in a zip file, which include the famous "f" circle logo, the equally famous Facebook thumb icon, and a "Find Us on Facebook."

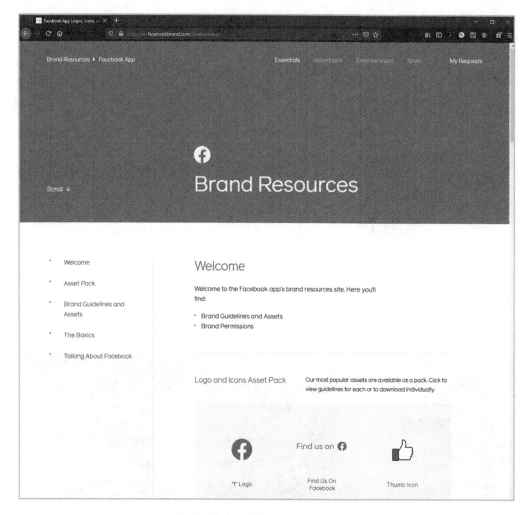

FIGURE 5–5. Download Facebook logos and icons

You must click on the checkbox below the icons to acknowledge that you read and accept the usage guidelines before you can download the icons.

■ Scroll down to learn more about the icon usage guidelines, which include how to use the "f" icon, keep enough space around the icons, and use only the Facebook-approved icons in the zip file.

■ You'll also learn what not to do with the icons, which includes changing their color, shape, or proportions.

If the Facebook Brand Resources page doesn't have the information you need, click the Get In Touch link at the bottom of the page to email the Facebook brand resources team.

LinkedIn

The LinkedIn Brand website gives you an overview of LinkedIn's brand system, including their logo, font, and color palette. You can download LinkedIn icons by clicking the Download Logo link shown in Figure 5–6 below, but you should click the Policies link next to it and read through their rules first.

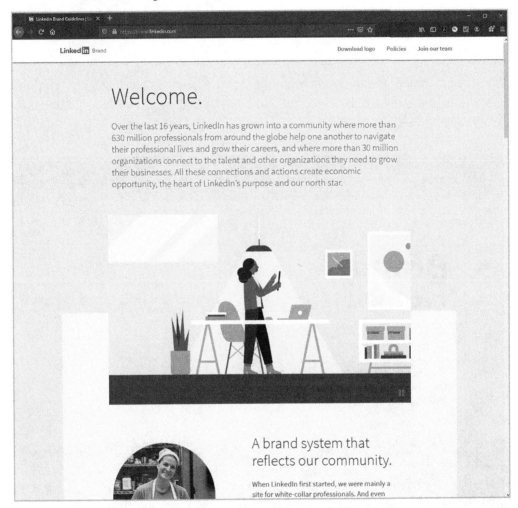

FIGURE 5–6. The LinkedIn Brand website

Here are some important points you should know about using the LinkedIn icons properly:

- Though you can change the size of the logo, you can't enlarge it beyond its native size or shrink it smaller than 21 pixels high.
- Don't change the color of the icon.

- You can use text along with the LinkedIn icon as long as the words are in a different font and color (preferably black) and the text leaves plenty of clear space around the icon.

If you have any other questions or have a specific use for the icon not covered on the site, contact the LinkedIn brand, communications, and social impact team at trademark@linkedin.com.

Twitter

The Twitter Brand Resources website shown in Figure 5-7 below gives you the opportunity to download the Twitter brand guidelines as well as various graphic files, including Twitter icons.

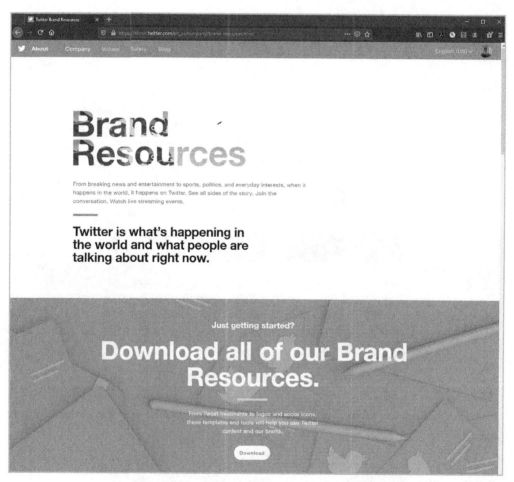

FIGURE 5-7. The Twitter Brand Resources website

Twitter provides its distinctive blue-and-white icons in EPS, SVG, PNG, and Adobe PSD formats. In addition to format requirements that are similar to the ones on Facebook and LinkedIn, you'll find some that are very specific to Twitter, including:

- Don't animate the icon so it talks, chirps, and/or flies.
- Don't add other birds or animals around the icon.
- Don't add "special features" such as cartoon thought bubbles to the icon.
- Don't anthropomorphize the icon—that is, don't give the Twitter bird human characteristics.

Twitter doesn't make it easy to contact them with your questions on the Twitter Brand Resources web page. You have to look in the fine print within the Agreement section at the bottom of the page to find the email address link, which is trademarks@ twitter.com. If you open or download the Brand Guidelines PDF document on the web page, you can also click the email address link on the last page.

YouTube

Before you can use YouTube icons for your website or other marketing tools, such as your email signature, you must review the information on the YouTube Brand Resources website, shown in Figure 5–8 on page 72. Then you need to click on the Fill Out a Brand Use Request Form link at the top or bottom of the page to get permission to use the icon.

If you've already used icons for Facebook, LinkedIn, Twitter, or Instagram, then you'll be familiar with many of YouTube's restrictions, including not altering the icon. However, if you're thinking about changing the icon's size, you need to be familiar with the density-independent pixel (dp) measurement. YouTube requires the icon to be no smaller than 24 dp.

The form also requires you to create and attach a PDF file containing an overview of your request (which you can create easily in your favorite word processor) as well as screenshots or mockups of how the icon will appear in your website, social networking websites, and other places like an email signature. This is just a partial list; you can read the form to learn what else you need to submit.

> **TIP**
>
> The dp measurement is based on screen resolution; 1dp is the equivalent of 1 pixel on a 160-dpi (dots per inch) screen. You can get the dpi equivalent for that size by using a dpi calculator such as DPI Love. Once you know the screen's dpi, you can send this information to YouTube when you fill out the Brand Use Request Form.

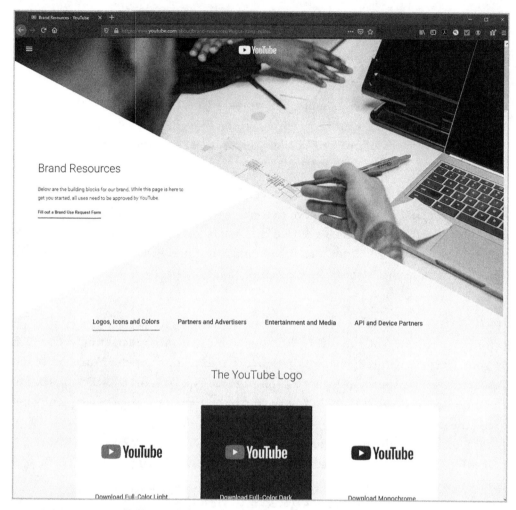

FIGURE 5–8. The YouTube Brand Resources website

Instagram

To access the Instagram logo, you can visit their Brand Resources page.

You can add the Instagram logo to your website, email signature, and marketing materials so long as it is not the most prominent logo and doesn't convey any partnership between you and Instagram. You must also keep the "I" in Instagram capitalized whenever you reference it.

For more information on using Instagram's logo in large-scale marketing or broadcast, refer to the link above.

VIDEO REQUIREMENTS

Today's social networking websites allow you to add video to your social networking profiles so you can further engage with people in your own profile and your business profile, and/or use video in your advertising. One-third of online activity is spent watching video, so if you want to upload video to your profiles, you need to know the requirements for each social networking website.

We took the information for video requirements on the five social networking websites we cover in this chapter from the Sprout Social website. We found some of this information was out of date when we were writing the book, so we updated the specifications as of early 2020.

However, sites' requirements can change rapidly, so it's always best to consult the help pages on the social networking sites themselves if you run into any problems.

Facebook

The most common types of video shared on Facebook are in link posts, Facebook Stories, and desktop newsfeed ads. Facebook recommends that you upload your videos in MP4 or MOV format, but you can also upload them in many other formats. You can view the entire list of supported formats on the Facebook Help Center.

Posts

Here are the requirements (and a couple of recommendations) for adding video to your newsfeed posts:

- Facebook recommends that you use a resolution of 1280 pixels wide by 720 pixels high for videos in landscape orientation or 720 pixels wide by 1280 pixels high for portrait orientation. Implicit in this recommendation is that if you upload a video with different dimensions, the video may look fuzzy and you'll have to fix it.
- If you upload a smaller video, the minimum width is 600 pixels.
- The file size for your video must be no larger than 4GB, the frame rate must be no more than 30fps, and it can run no longer than 120 minutes (two hours).

TIP

A video in landscape orientation has an aspect ratio of 16:9, and, as you probably guessed, a video in portrait orientation has an aspect ratio of 9:16. The Facebook mobile app renders both types to an aspect ratio of 2:3, so be sure to test your video in both desktop/laptop and mobile views before you upload it.

Facebook Stories

Facebook Stories looks much different from the normal Facebook newsfeed, so it's no surprise that it has different video specifications, too:

TIP

The requirements for ads in Facebook Stories are the same as the ones given above.

- The minimum video dimensions must be 500 pixels wide by 500 pixels high.
- Facebook recommends an aspect ratio ranging from 1.91 to 9:16. If your video has an aspect ratio lower than 9:16, Stories automatically adds colored gradient bars on the top and bottom, and the text you add when you upload your video appears below it.
- The video file can be no larger than 4GB, and it cannot play for more than two minutes.

Newsfeed Ads

If you really want attention that newsfeed video just can't give you, you can purchase Facebook ads that appear either in users' newsfeeds or in the right column of the Facebook newsfeed screen. No matter how you choose to display your ad, you need to follow these rules:

- Videos in landscape orientation must be 1280 pixels wide by 720 pixels high, with an aspect ratio of 16:9.
- The minimum required video dimensions are 600 pixels wide by 315 pixels high, with a 1.9:1 aspect ratio.
- For square ads, size the video to 600 pixels wide by 600 pixels wide, with a 1:1 aspect ratio.
- The video file must not be larger than 4GB, must not have more than a 30fps frame rate, and must not run longer than 120 minutes.

LinkedIn

LinkedIn has different requirements for videos placed in newsfeed posts than ones that appear in paid ads. We'll give you a rundown of the most important information here. However, if you want a complete list of specifications, including video link sharing and different types of video ads, go to the LinkedIn Marketing Solutions website.

TIP

You need to use the same video requirements listed below for an advertising video that appears in the right column. However, Facebook will shrink that video to fit. That should help you determine how you want to present your video ad.

Posts

Before you start uploading video, be sure that you're using an approved video format. Formats LinkedIn accepts include:

- ASF
- AVI
- FLV
- MOV
- MP4
- VP8
- VP9
- WMV2
- WMV3
- MPEG-1
- MPEG-4
- MKV
- WebM

TIP

The video file size has to be at least 75KB and no larger than 5GB. This may determine the video format you use.

Once you decide which format you want to use, here are the other requirements you need to know:

- The video must be no shorter than three seconds and no longer than ten minutes.
- The resolution can be anywhere from 256 pixels wide by 144 pixels high for small videos and 4096 pixels wide by 2304 pixels high for large ones.
- Aspect ratios can be between 1:2.4 or 2.4:1.
- Frame rates must be between 10fps and 60 fps with bit rates from 192 kbps to 30 Mbps.

Ads

Ads appear differently within LinkedIn so they can get readers' attention more easily. To accomplish this, LinkedIn has more specific video requirements for ads:

- LinkedIn Ads only supports videos in landscape or square orientation.
- Videos in square orientation (that is, with a 1:1 aspect ratio) need to be no smaller than 600 pixels wide by 600 pixels high (aka 600 pixels square) and no larger than 1080 pixels square.
- The video must be three seconds to 30 minutes long.

TIP

The file size needs to be no smaller than 75KB and no larger than 200MB.

- The frame rate must be less than 30fps.
- LinkedIn Ads only accepts video files in MP4 format.

Twitter

Twitter has different video requirements for placing a video in a tweet than for putting one in your paid display ad.

A Video in Your Tweet

If you want to upload a video in your tweet, here's how to format your video before you upload it to Twitter:

- If you want people to view your video on the web or on the Twitter mobile app, your files in MP4 format must include H264 compression and the AAC (Advanced Audio Coding) audio format.
- Videos must be no longer than 2 minutes and 20 seconds long, and the file must be no larger than 512MB.
- The video frame rate must be no more than 40fps and the bitrate must be no more than 25 Mbps.

> **TIP**
>
> You can upload the video in MOV format if you want it to appear only on the mobile app.

- The minimum resolution must be 32 pixels wide by 32 pixels high.
- Maximum resolution in landscape orientation is 1920 pixels wide by 1200 pixels high. In portrait orientation, the maximum resolution is 1200 pixels wide by 1920 pixels high.
- The aspect ratio must be anywhere between 1:2.39 to 2.39:1.

Ads

As with ads on Facebook and LinkedIn, Twitter ad videos have different requirements than videos uploaded to a tweet:

- You can upload the video in three orientations:
  - Landscape at 1280 pixels wide by 720 pixels high
  - Portrait at 720 pixels wide by 1280 pixels high
  - Square at 720 pixels wide by 720 pixels high

> **TIP**
>
> The maximum running time, as with videos uploaded to a tweet, is 2 minutes and 20 seconds. However, select advertisers can increase their video run time by as much as ten minutes, but you have to request that extension from Twitter.

- The file type can be in MP4 or MOV formats.
- The aspect ratio can be 16:9 for landscape orientation, 9:16 for portrait orientation, or 1:1 for square orientation.
- The video file size can be no larger than 1GB.
- The video parameters include H264 High Profile compression, AAC-LC audio, a frame rate no higher than 30fps, and a video bit rate of no more than 5 Mbps.

YouTube

As with any other social media website, there are differences between videos on your YouTube channel and ads you post on YouTube for everyone to see. However, since YouTube is meant for videos, you will obviously have more options—and restrictions.

Channel Video Requirements

Your uploaded videos will play in a 16:9 aspect ratio. If your video doesn't use this ratio, such as one filmed in portrait orientation, the player will try to adjust the video to your aspect ratio and the size of the viewer's device.

In some cases, YouTube adds padding around the video to fit within the viewing window. Padding is white in regular viewing mode and dark gray in Dark theme viewing mode.

If you want to create videos in 16:9 aspect ratio, keep the following specifications in mind for filming videos at specific resolutions:

- 2160p: 3840 pixels wide by 2160 pixels high
- 1440p: 2560 pixels wide by 1440 pixels high
- 1080p: 1920 pixels wide by 1080 pixels high
- 720p: 1280 pixels wide by 720 pixels high
- 480p: 854 pixels wide by 480 pixels high
- 360p: 640 pixels wide by 360 pixels high
- 240p: 426 pixels wide by 240 pixels high

> **TIP**
>
> Don't add padding or black bars to your video, because that affects YouTube's ability to change the video size. How your video appears on the site may not be what you're looking for.

If you're wondering what format you should save your video in, YouTube accepts a large number of types:

- MOV
- MPEG4
- MP4
- AVI
- WMV

- MPEGPS
- FLV
- 3GPP
- WebM
- DNxHR
- ProRes
- CineForm
- HEVC (H.265)

TIP

You can learn more about uploading videos to YouTube on the Video Resolution & Aspect Ratios web page in the YouTube Help Center.

Display Ad Requirements

If you want to post display ads on YouTube, you have to qualify for the YouTube Partner Program (YPP), which allows users to make money from their videos if they meet certain requirements. As of November 2019, YouTube requires that you have at least 1,000 subscribers and 4,000 watch hours of your channel by the public over the past 12 months. Four thousand watch hours means that all the people who view your channel should have watched one or more videos for a cumulative total of 4,000 hours or more. You can learn how to get your watch time report by reading the Watch Time Report page in the YouTube Help Center.

Because YouTube changes its interface occasionally, like all social networking websites, you'll have to see where the display ads appear when you use YouTube. If you're thinking about display ads, here are the rules for video ads:

- When you view a display ad, all you see is a static cover image that's usually an attractive frame from the video. Some images appear in a larger version and some in a smaller one, so you need two cover images: the larger size at 300 pixels wide by 250 pixels high and the smaller size at 300 pixels wide by 60 pixels high.
- The aspect ratio for the video must be 16:9.
- The maximum size of the video is 128GB.
- A video must not last longer than 12 hours.
- The maximum dimensions depend on the video's resolution, which is usually tied to one's monitor resolution. Here are the recommended dimensions for the minimum 240p resolution to the maximum 2160p resolution, in terms of pixel width by pixel height:
  - 240p: 426 pixels wide by 240 pixels high
  - 360p: 640 pixels wide by 360 pixels high
  - 480p: 854 pixels wide by 480 pixels high
  - 720p: 1280 pixels wide by 720 pixels high
  - 1080p: 1920 pixels wide by 1080 pixels high

TIP

You can get more information about the YPP on the YouTube Partner Program Overview & Eligibility page in the YouTube Help Center.

- 1440p: 2560 pixels wide by 1440 pixels high
- 2160p: 3840 pixels wide by 2160 pixels high

■ YouTube accepts display ad videos in a variety of formats, but not as many as for videos posted to your channel:

- MOV
- MPEG4
- MP4
- AVI
- WMV
- MPEGPS
- FLV
- 3GPP
- WebM

TIP

You may have noticed that the recommended height and the resolution are the same because a video's resolution is determined by the height of the pixels supported in your computer's screen resolution.

Other Types of Ads

If you're not interested in a display ad, YouTube offers four other types of ads that you can make money from under certain conditions:

■ *Skippable*. This video appears before, during, or after you play a video. After five seconds, the user can skip watching the rest of the ad. The good news about this type is that it's the only one of the four listed in this section that allows you to get money no matter what device the viewer uses to watch the ad.

■ *Nonskippable*. This ad plays for 15 seconds, and the viewer must watch it all. You can place this ad before, during, or after another video. YouTube doesn't give you any money from viewers who watch this ad on TVs or game consoles, but you do get money from viewers on computers and smartphones.

■ *Midroll*. This ad is played during viewing of another video that's longer than 10 minutes, much like a commercial on TV. You can determine where you want the ad to appear within the longer video, or you can tell YouTube to place the midroll ad automatically. Viewers can skip a midroll ad after 30 seconds. As with nonskippable ads, YouTube doesn't give you money from people who watch the ad on a TV or game console, but gives you money from viewers on computers and smartphones.

■ *Bumper*. This ad plays before the content and is only six seconds long. The viewer can't skip the ad, and it's ideal for viewing videos on mobile devices because of the ad's short run time.

Now that you know about the different types of ads you can create, many of the requirements and accepted formats are the same for a posted video as they are for a display ad. However, there are some other specifications you should know before you start creating your video:

- The maximum video length for skippable ads is 12 hours. (Chances are that your video won't be this long, but you can rest easy knowing YouTube figured it out.) Remember, the viewer can skip the ad after five seconds, so make those first five seconds memorable enough to keep them watching.
- Midroll video ads have a minimum 30-second running time.
- Bumper video ads can be no longer than six seconds.

Instagram

Instagram is a heavily visual platform, and you would expect videos to perform well there. Since videos autoplay in the feed, they can be very appealing and generate many views for your post.

Feed Post Videos

In the regular feed, you have three options for video sizes:

- A square video in a 1:1 aspect ratio is still the go-to format, since the platform was designed around square content
- Vertical videos are supported up to a 4:5 ratio. If your video is taller than this, it will get cropped down to fit.
- Horizontal videos are best shot in a 16:9 ratio, which is what you get when you film with your mobile device turned to landscape mode.

Those are just the ratios (with the width being the first number and the height being the second number). But the actual size of the video (in pixels) can vary depending on your content. Ideally, you want nothing smaller than 320 pixels; the maximum is 1080 pixels. For videos, you want to get as close to the 1080-pixel limit as possible to ensure your video comes through in the highest quality.

Story Videos

Story posts are formatted in a 9:16 vertical orientation. If you want your video to fill the screen of the Story, it will need to be in a 9:16 ratio and ideally 1080 pixels wide by 1920 pixels high. However, you're not restricted to that option. You can upload a video of any size or shape and pinch-and-zoom it to fit it anywhere on the screen.

Instagram Live Videos

Instagram Live can only be filmed on your mobile device within the Instagram app; you can't upload these videos from any other source. The app will always record your videos in a 9:16 vertical orientation.

IGTV Videos

Similar to Stories, IGTV is designed for a 9:16 format, with the same 1080-by-1920-pixel video. The app will also support videos in a 4:5 and 1:1 ratio, though. And, good news! While IGTV used to only support vertical video, you can now upload horizontal videos in the 16:9 orientation as well.

LINK REQUIREMENTS

It's easy to copy hyperlinks from one website and paste them into a post you're writing on a social networking website. Today's social networks also provide short previews of your link to entice more people to click on it.

Social networking websites either truncate a link in the post if it's too long or use their own built-in link-shortening technologies to make the link meet their requirements. If you think a website link (for example, from an online retailer) is too long, you can also use a link-shortening website such as Bitly.

Facebook

Though you don't technically need to include the http:// or https:// prefixes when you share a link in a Facebook post, go ahead and do so to make sure Facebook can insert a preview in your post. (Better safe than sorry.) Fortunately, when you select the URL in your browser address bar, the entire URL is copied. So when you paste the URL into your post, you should see the preview that contains the page title, the opening text in the link, and the first graphic in the linked web page.

> **TIP**
>
> After Facebook adds the thumbnail preview graphic to your post, you can delete the URL from your post. Then your viewers can simply click on the preview graphic to visit the site.

LinkedIn

Your LinkedIn post can have as many as 1,300 characters, but LinkedIn has built-in link-shortening technology, to save most of those 1,300 characters for your message. What's more, the site also allows you to share your posts with Twitter, with its 280-character limit, so keeping your URLs short is a must. (Of course, if you do share your post with Twitter, you need to keep the whole thing under its character limit.)

When you share a link to your website, such as to a new blog post, it's a good practice to have your company URL in your link so your post reinforces your brand. However, LinkedIn automatically shortens a link longer than 26 characters, including the required http:// or https:// prefixes.

So if you have a URL longer than 26 characters, you won't see your company URL but a LinkedIn-supplied link such as https://lnkd.in/bRXcYDb. You'll still see the preview that links to your website, but your company URL won't appear in your post.

Twitter

You only have 280 characters to work with in a tweet, and some of that text is taken up by your link. Twitter uses an automatic link-shortening app called t.co. This app not only shortens your link to maximize the number of characters you can type in your tweet, but it also checks the linked site for any malware or other dangers.

The t.co app makes any link 23 characters long (even if the original link is shorter) and automatically truncates any links that are longer with an ellipsis (. . .) at the end of the link. So you still have 254 characters to work with. And if you use a link in your tweet, you can't opt out of link shortening.

YouTube

YouTube doesn't give you very many limitations when you paste a link into your video description. Unlike LinkedIn and Twitter, YouTube doesn't use a built-in link-shortening app, so your links can include your company name to reinforce your brand. However, YouTube will truncate any URLs that are longer than 40 characters with an ellipsis (. . .) and requires the http:// or https:// prefix.

Instagram

Instagram does not support the use of links in regular feed posts. A URL included in a caption will appear as plain text and will not be clickable or accessible to your followers.

You can place a single link in your profile bio. To edit this link, go to your profile (by clicking the person icon in the bottom navigation menu on your mobile device) and tap the Edit Profile button. In the Website field, you can type (or copy and paste) any URL you wish to direct visitors to.

If you have an Instagram business account with more than 10,000 followers, you can add a URL to a Story post. To do this, tap on the chain-link icon on your story during the creation stage and paste your URL into the Link field. This will allow viewers to click or swipe on the story to go directly to that link.

Now that you know how to format your posts on the five most important social media websites, we're going to spend some time discussing how to create images in Chapter 6 and video in Chapter 7, so you're prepared to design more effective media for social networks.

Create Images for Social Media

I mages are the heart and soul of social media.

While video is tremendously engaging and highly effective at establishing trust, and text continues to be the backbone of communicating online, imagery plays a crucial role.

Consider for a moment just how prevalent the use of images is. Facebook, Twitter, LinkedIn, Pinterest, and Instagram all natively support posting pictures, not to mention sharing them privately in direct messages. What's more, every social network allows users to upload a custom profile image—a way to visually represent themselves to the world.

Facebook, LinkedIn, and Twitter allow users to upload images that appear above their profiles as profile and cover photos, as you read in Chapter 5. Even YouTube, a network driven by video uploads, uses them, and even allows custom images as thumbnails for uploaded videos.

All that is to illustrate that no matter when or how someone chooses to engage with you or your content on social media, they will see one or more images that you've chosen to incorporate.

The imagery you employ on social media is often one of the first things your audience sees, and it's your first chance to make an outstanding impression. This chapter is designed to help you make the absolute most of that opportunity. It starts with understanding the subjective quality of the imagery you might use, according to the network you're posting to; then we'll review how to find and create those images.

DETERMINE IMAGE CRITERIA

The first consideration for what makes a "good" image is understanding the medium in which that image is going to be published, used, and consumed. If it's for a profile photo, how does it look on a small mobile device? If it's going to be shared in an Instagram post, does it conform to that network's size and ratio requirements?

As we discussed in Chapter 5, every network has its own image requirements and restrictions. And since these can change at any time, whenever you create a new image, you should check the website's help center for the latest specifications or use a predefined template in your favorite image editor (more on these in a bit).

For now, it's sufficient to have a general understanding of the networks' current preferences:

Posts that appear in the feed—the normal stream of posts—for Facebook, LinkedIn, and Twitter should be landscape, as are cover photos. Feed posts for Instagram should be square. Feed posts for Pinterest should be profile. Story content for the networks that support Stories should also be portrait, and profile images should be square.

While most networks will allow you to upload images that aren't optimally designed, that will typically give you poor results.

What does that mean? For starters, it might result in an image being cropped or stretched or scaled so that it no longer appears how you intended. If you create a tall portrait image with important text at the top and bottom and share it in a tweet, only the center will likely be displayed in the feed—your text won't be shown unless someone clicks on the image!

Furthermore, if an uploaded image is really small, it may be stretched, reducing its quality and appearance. Low-quality images are not appealing and therefore not eye-catching. Which sounds better to you, a blurry picture of some trees, or a crisp photo of a mountain valley where the lake and forest are in sharp detail?

Which do you think is more likely to stop people from idly scrolling past it?

One important consideration when it comes to imagery is communication strength and preference—both yours and your audience's. Some people are naturally more comfortable and gifted when it comes to communication, including written, spoken, and graphic design. Stephanie has worked over her lifetime to develop her verbal communication skills, while Mike is a natural-born writer. If you find it challenging to create interesting images, consider finding someone whose strengths can complement you in that area.

Similarly, some people prefer to learn through reading, listening, or watching. These learning styles carry additional nuance depending on how information is presented. Some members of your audience, for instance, may need to understand the big picture before you dive into the details of a topic, whereas others may prefer a structured, step-by-step approach.

This is the intersection where good design lives, a nexus between the creator's skill and understanding of their audience and the perceptual needs of those viewers.

Sorry. We tend to nerd out over the psychological impact and effectiveness of good marketing.

The point, though, is this: A "good" image is highly subjective. It should reflect you and/or your brand in some way, convey your message, and speak to your audience. That may sound vague and unhelpful, so let's explore briefly what makes for a *bad* image.

First and foremost, images have to be high quality. Unintentional blurriness, graininess, obvious stock images, clip art . . . remember, any image you share publicly will be a representation of your brand and possibly the first and only impression you make on someone. Make it count!

Second, never use other people's copyright-protected images. It's illegal, and the last thing you want is for your brand to be publicly humiliated for your poor decision.

Third, it's very important to have a sense of your brand's style, tone, and voice, and avoid images that do not fit that. For instance, it's always OK to have a sense of humor, but if you're representing a professional product or service, filling your feed with joke memes is not a good idea.

If you always try to find or create great images that align with your brand style, you'll be in good shape. But where do those images come from?

HOW TO FIND GREAT IMAGES

There are basically three ways that you can generate images for social media (speaking mostly about feed posts at this point):

1. Purchase images
2. Create graphics
3. Photograph your own

Now, when we talk about purchasing images, that doesn't necessarily mean they have to be expensive. There are even places you can get images for free—but they have to be designated as available for your use. Using Google's image search is not acceptable unless you go to Google's advanced settings and scroll down to set parameters for usage rights to be "free to use or share, even commercially." Even then, be careful! Being sued for copyright infringement is not fun, and you could get in trouble for using an image that someone *else* illegally shared. It is worth the effort to use those other sites.

Pixabay, for instance, is a great place to source free imagery that you can use in your marketing and social media posts. However, any time you use an image, you are typically required to give credit to the source of that image, which may or may not be convenient. Instead, we recommend purchasing images from repositories like Shutterstock, iStock, or Depositphotos.

Usually you can invest in "credits" upfront and use them to buy and download images whenever you need. This is particularly convenient when a site offers a sale on bulk credits at a discount, so watch for those!

There are two major benefits to buying images. First, you're purchasing the right to use that image on social media and in marketing materials, so you know all your activities will be legal. Second, by paying for an image, you're adding a layer of exclusivity to your design. More people will be likely to use a free image, meaning there's a greater chance of that photo turning up in someone else's marketing. By paying for your image, you make that less likely. (You also know that the image you're paying for will be high-quality.)

The second option is to create the graphics yourself. We'll go into some tools you can use for this in a moment, but the idea is simple. Instead of a picture someone else took, you can create a graphic that uses shapes, textures, icons, and text to communicate your message. These can be as simple as a few words of text on a white background, or as complex as a tall infographic that illustrates a series of facts and figures to tell a story.

While you will obviously need a minimal level of design skill, this is an approach that is worth exploring! You can also consider using an outside graphic design service or working with a freelance designer from Fiverr to create one or more images or even templates for you to use again and again.

The third approach, and perhaps the best one, is to create your own imagery and photography. This is an inexpensive way for you to create amazing images that align perfectly with your brand.

All it requires is a camera—these days your smartphone will do just fine—and some forethought. What can you photograph? What will you be talking about on social media where specific images would be a great addition?

Here are ten things you might consider photographing for your posts:

1. Yourself
2. Your staff
3. Your business and facilities
4. Nature

5. Your city
6. Your customers
7. Your target audience
8. Your hobbies and interests
9. Events
10. Your industry

If you've never done much photography, take a day to watch some YouTube videos on composition and techniques, particularly those related to your camera of choice. Peter McKinnon is one of our favorite photographers to follow—you'll learn a lot from his videos!

For instance, with a newer iPhone in portrait mode, you can capture some amazing close-up images, allowing the phone to automatically apply bokeh (blur) to the background, giving the item you're photographing additional focus.

Let's say you have a local plumbing service—not generally considered a particularly photogenic business. But what if you grabbed your phone and spent a day taking interesting and unique shots of shiny new plumbing? Shots of pipes up close or even shots taken looking through the pipe!

Routinely taking an hour or two for business photography can create a library of "stock photos" that will last you and your brand for years.

SOCIAL MEDIA IMAGERY BEST PRACTICES

Given how easy it is to create brand imagery today, you must create a set of standards for yourself and apply them every time you post. Never let an image be shared to your social channel that doesn't meet your high standards. Make no mistake: One subpar image that is seen by your audience can have a detrimental impact on your brand. At best, your fans will ignore the post, and the network's algorithm will take that as a cue to reduce the reach of your next post. And at worst, you could injure your reputation among your fans.

So how do you go about creating a set of standards for your brand imagery?

In addition to the recommendations above, consider the following.

Apply Consistent Branding

Make sure that whenever you use fonts or colors or your logo in your images, you're consistent across all your properties. This is where it would be helpful to establish a style guide, even if it's just a Google Doc or Evernote that lists your established fonts and brand colors.

Consider including:

- Wide logo
- Square logo
- Black and white logo
- Logo usage and restrictions
- Headline/title font
- Body/normal text font
- Accent font
- Font weight and size, if appropriate
- Primary brand colors
- Secondary brand colors

Many of the tools we're going to talk about in a moment let you establish a brand kit so it's easy to be consistent when creating or editing.

Use a Logo or Watermark When Necessary

Along the same lines as consistent branding is the idea of putting your logo or watermark on your imagery. For photographers, this is an absolute must. For other businesses, though, a word of caution: Be judicious about your use of logos or watermarks on imagery, particularly on social media, because:

1. It adds more text to the image, and
2. It can potentially distract from the point of the image.

When considering whether to edit an image, ask yourself, "Does the logo detract from the image?" And, "Am I really afraid that someone else might use this image?" One example where it might make sense to include a logo or watermark is on product photography.

Use Less Text

You may be tempted at first to include lots of text on your imagery. For instance, if you are creating imagery for a sale campaign, you may want to put all the campaign details on the image, such as what discount you are offering and for how long. However, the more text you use, the more likely it will be perceived as an ad and dismissed before it's even read.

Because of that, Facebook used to have a guideline for ads called the "20 Percent Rule," which stated that no more than 20 percent of your image could contain text. They knew their users were not interested in images covered with text, and that would make the ad ineffective. Facebook has since relaxed that guideline, but the bias against text remains. If you intend to promote a post with an image on Facebook, include as little text as possible. Figure 6–1 below shows the difference a little less text can make.

FIGURE 6–1. A lot of text vs. a little text

The image on the left has way more text than it needs, whereas the image on the right has a simple headline and subhead that's enough to get attention.

Use Alternate Versions

We mentioned earlier that different networks support different image dimensions and aspect ratios. While it might seem like a pain to take an image you created for Facebook and create alternate versions for Instagram or for Stories, it is absolutely worth taking that time.

Using the wrong size and aspect ratio might not seem too terrible, until you realize that what you're missing is potential reach. A tall image shared in a Story will garner more attention as a thumbnail than a landscape image that only takes up a third of the available space. A too-small image that's shared to Facebook may be distorted and pixelated until it attracts no interest, as you can see in Figure 6–2 on page 92.

This is what it looks like when an image that's just 50 by 50 pixels is shared to Facebook. As you can see, the image quality is very poor, which doesn't achieve the goal of showing visitors what the product looks like.

FIGURE 6–2. A distorted image

RECOMMENDED TOOLS

And now, the moment you've been waiting for: How do you accomplish all this?

With the help of a few tools, of course.

These days, the tools and apps we have at our disposal are so powerful and inexpensive that using them to create your graphics will seem like magic!

We're going to review some specific tools before looking at some apps that you can use both on desktop and mobile devices. Depending on what you want to accomplish and your target audience, your smartphone may be all you need to create great imagery!

Image Capture

According to the old saying, the best camera is the one you have with you. And with today's smartphones, that has never been truer. The iPhone 11 Pro's camera is simply astounding (and subsequent models will likely continue to improve). You can take close-up shots, selfies, panoramas, and even live video! Android has similarly amazing options.

If you want to level up your photography with a DSLR camera, the Canon EOS Rebel T6i is an excellent starter camera. The reliable camera body will give you an opportunity to experiment with different lenses and techniques. Check out some of the bundles for sale online, where you can pick up a camera, a couple of lenses, and a boatload of equipment for less than $600.

Image Editing

The industry standard for image editing software is, of course, Adobe Photoshop. With time and patience, you can master all the amazing features that application brings to the table. Imagine being able to blend two images together, or remove any aspects of a photograph that detract from the focus—and so much more!

And today, Adobe Photoshop has never been more affordable, with great monthly payment options. You can simply subscribe online to the tool or tools you want (from the entire Adobe suite of products) and enjoy constant updates and features, like being able to save your work to the Adobe Cloud, where team members can collaborate on a project. There is, of course, a massive learning curve due to the power and complexity of the program. If you're willing to give it a go, have a few things in mind that you want to accomplish and start watching YouTube videos to see how it's done.

But if you don't want to learn Photoshop, there are alternatives. Photos, an image-editing app that is included with macOS, offers straightforward ways to crop, resize, and adjust the basic levels of an image. For PC, we recommend the free app, GIMP, which is remarkably powerful.

If you want to edit photos on your mobile device, check out Snapseed, an incredibly powerful app with a wide range of preset filters and enhancements, available for free for both Android and iOS devices. (There's also a mobile version of

Adobe Photoshop you can try that comes with your subscription and has much of the same functionality.)

Graphic Design

Canva, available online and as a mobile app, has become the industry standard for designing graphics online. While you can use more powerful applications like Adobe Illustrator if you have access and training, Canva is almost better for social media graphics because it's quick, easy to learn, and relatively inexpensive. Social media graphics are generally meant for one-time use; you don't want to spend hours creating a complex design, as you easily could in Adobe.

In fact, Canva offers a free use option in which the only charge is for the use of stock photos or graphics. There are loads of templates you can access based on all manner of typical sizes, making it incredibly convenient to create a graphic for Facebook, Twitter, Instagram, Pinterest, or LinkedIn. And once you have your graphic looking just the way you want, you can use the Resize option to make copies in all the other image formats you need.

A paid subscription adds a few more bells and whistles. Remember earlier, when we suggested you create a brand style guide? Canva helps you coordinate and save all those must-have brand elements in one place. When you upgrade to a paid subscription, you can save a Brand Kit, with specified fonts and colors and logos uploaded for future use. Not only is this a handy reference, but when adding text elements to a design, the element will automatically use your specified font, helping to ensure that consistency we spoke of earlier.

Canva is also great when used to support a team. Team members can share designs and previously uploaded elements, and completed designs are all accessible, making collaboration a cinch. New team members can be added for a nominal monthly fee.

A great alternative to Canva is Easil. It has many similar elements, such as selecting an image size to start, the option of choosing a template, and editing the key elements of that design visually.

> **TIP** ⓘ
>
> If you need to remove the background from an image, you can use Canva or Easil for that, as well as the site remove.bg.

We recommend you give both apps a try and see which one works better with your design ability, needs, and processes.

Armed with these tools, and the best practices outlined earlier, you're in a much better position to create amazing visual assets for your brand on social media. When you combine great photography with outstanding graphic design, your imagery will explode in effectiveness.

Practice these techniques and approaches. Get feedback from teammates and peers. Like writing, great imagery is simply not optional, but it can be learned and improved on over time. In our next chapter, we're going to tackle the ultimate media for driving engagement and building brand awareness and authority: video.

Chapter 7

Create Video for Social Media

According to Wyzowl's 2019 "The State of Video Marketing Survey," 79 percent of consumers say a brand's video has persuaded them to buy software or an app. Are you interested in reaching that huge audience by leveraging video for your own brand and business?

Let's share one more statistic with you first, though: According to a 2017 survey by Livestream, 80 percent of consumers would prefer to watch live videos from a brand than read a blog.

Consumers today have embraced the idea of watching video to learn about a topic, a product, or a brand. Live video, in particular, has evolved into more than just an option for savvy marketers—it's a requirement for virtually any business that wants to stand out.

But even with live video you have lots of options. This chapter will help you determine which platform or platforms to use, whether to use live or recorded video, short or long, solo or guests . . . or all of the above!

One of the great benefits of video is that it's really quite flexible. Your video strategy might include a regular live broadcast plus shorter recorded segments. You can start on one platform and then branch out to simulcasting on multiple social networks.

You can take your time to explore what approach works best for both you and your audience. What matters is that you find a way to integrate video into your social media strategy—because it drives your customers to take action.

So to start this chapter, let's look at exactly why video is so effective so that you can create the best possible video content for your brand. We'll then review how to post video to social networks (covered in Chapter 5), discuss the advantages and disadvantages of live vs. recorded and short vs. long, and even address specific gear and other recommendations.

WHY VIDEO IS EFFECTIVE

We mentioned at the beginning of this chapter a couple of motivating statistics that any CEO or CMO should read and immediately approve your video budget request. But there's one more very important statistic we need to add:

Zero percent of consumers buy from bad videos.

Technically we made that one up, but you get the idea, right? If you've ever seen a really, really, *really* bad commercial—like the ones that run on late-night cable TV—you know how ineffective they are.

Fortunately, creating good—or even great—video is possible for any brand. So it's worth taking a moment to explore what makes video so effective. Understanding this will help you craft video content that resonates, engages, and ultimately converts your customers.

The Power of Visuals

As the saying goes, a picture is worth a thousand words. That's because our brains are wired to process visual information (like a picture) faster and with more depth than mere words. Consider then that video is basically 30 to 60 images (frames) every second. If each frame is communicating a thousand words, that's at least 1.8 million words in just a minute!

Look around you for a moment. Whether you're sitting in a Starbucks or on the couch in your home, your eyes and brain can process a ton of information instantaneously.

Close your eyes and picture what you were just looking at in your mind.

No one had to tell you what color the walls were or what pieces of furniture were in the room or who else was there. Your brain captured all that information for you. Now consider how long it would have taken someone to describe that scene to you.

When it comes to videos for your business, you can leverage how quickly human brains are wired to process visual information by doing things like making eye contact or filming yourself in a professional location. Those simple things can help you establish trust and authority without saying a single word.

Visual Plus *Audio!*

Because video includes both visual and audio components, it's actually far easier to elicit desired emotional responses like trust. That's important because, according to researchers at the University of Southern California, the most successful marketing campaigns include at least 31 percent emotional content—that is, aspects of the information being conveyed that are relatable, likable, or evoke an emotion of some kind in the audience.

So what is it about video that makes it so effective at communicating emotional content?

Back in the 1960s, psychology professor Albert Mehrabian conducted studies into human communication patterns at UCLA. As a result of two of those studies, we now have a famously misunderstood "rule" that "communication is only 7 percent verbal and 93 percent nonverbal. The nonverbal component [is] made up of body language (55 percent) and tone of voice (38 percent)." While Mehrabian was studying only the effect of a single word, not entire speeches, there is certainly an element of truth to this rule.

Whatever the exact ratios, we clearly communicate more through body language and tone of voice than through words, which is why videos can be so effective. We can speak calmly and infuse our words with positive energy and excitement. We can let our audience see how much we care about them and about what we're saying.

Brand Recall

According to Insivia, "Viewers retain 95 percent of a message when they watch it in a video compared to 10 percent when reading it in text."

Those numbers will vary, of course, depending on the viewer and the content of the video, but your audience will tend to remember your video content exponentially more than your written content, including your overall brand.

If you successfully and consistently incorporate brand imagery and messaging throughout your videos, you will see a noticeable "brand lift" across all your channels, as the repetition of your brand identity will be *brand*-ed into your audience's memory.

When someone who has seen your videos spots a tweeted link to one of your blog posts, they'll be more likely to click through to read it. When someone sees one of your social media ads, they'll be inclined to learn more because you've already established trust through consistent content and messaging.

That brings us to the last huge benefit video offers . . .

Frequency Illusion

Have you ever noticed that the day after you drive a new car off the lot, it seems like everyone else around you suddenly owns the same car? Don't worry—it's not a conspiracy. It's actually an illusion—a misperception that plays out in our minds due to a new or renewed awareness of something.

It's called *frequency illusion* (aka the Baader-Meinhof phenomenon), and brands that successfully pursue video content as part of their social media strategy are uniquely positioned to leverage this phenomenon.

We've already stated that video content is a more powerful medium than text for establishing brand recall. This means that once someone watches just one of your videos, they're more likely to remember you and your brand the next time they see marketing from your company. To them, it will seem as though your brand is suddenly everywhere, whereas in truth they're just noticing it now that your video has made an impression. The more videos you create and post, the more often you'll enjoy the benefits of this phenomenon.

More practically, once you start creating video content, you can take advantage of social network algorithms as well as retargeting. Here's what we mean by that.

If one of your followers on Facebook/Twitter/LinkedIn watches and engages with one of your live videos, the network will see that activity and will be more likely to serve that follower more of your posts in the future, video or otherwise.

This is why it is so important as a video creator or show host to ask engaging questions of your viewers, such as, "Where are you watching from?" and, "Do you have any other questions for our guest?" These prompts to leave comments not only keep your viewers engaged and interested, but they also help pave the way for the networks to insert future posts into their feeds.

And if you're adding a paid advertising element to your social media marketing (which we'll dig into in Chapter 9), you can actually target viewers of your videos with related ads. Imagine being able to broadcast a video on a specific issue and then following it up with ads promoting a related article on your site that can convert those viewers into subscribers.

That's powerful!

When you combine video with the other social media marketing techniques we cover in this book, you really can achieve a convincing "frequency illusion" and get people buzzing about how your brand seems to be everywhere.

That said, let's go over some very specific ways to create and leverage video content on social media, focusing on the platforms and tools that are widely available.

PUBLISHING AND BROADCASTING SOCIAL VIDEO

In Chapter 5, we discussed the specific video requirements and capabilities of the top five social networking websites, so let's briefly summarize how things stand as of our publication date:

1. *Facebook*: You may upload recorded video and broadcast live video to personal profiles, business pages, and groups.
2. *Twitter*: You may upload recorded video and broadcast live video (via Periscope).
3. *LinkedIn*: You may upload recorded video and broadcast live video to personal profiles and business pages. Note that access to LinkedIn Live is limited and requires LinkedIn approval.
4. *Instagram*: You may upload recorded video and broadcast live video to personal and business profiles.
5. *YouTube*: You may upload recorded video and broadcast live video.

Facebook, Twitter, Instagram, and YouTube can broadcast live video from mobile, which means you can stream from anywhere. For a higher-quality stream, you can broadcast from desktop to Facebook, Twitter, and YouTube, where you can use a nice webcam or even a DSLR camera that offers better video quality than your mobile device.

LinkedIn Live requires a third-party app to broadcast, such as Switcher Studio or StreamYard (both of which charge a monthly fee). You can also use these apps or others (e.g., Ecamm Live, OBS Studio) to broadcast to multiple platforms simultaneously while adding branding and effects, such as a watermarked logo or transitions between cameras.

Which is to say, you have a lot of options! You can do live video from your phone or record and publish video content to whichever social platform(s) best meets your needs and suits your audience.

Remember, always check the help centers on the social networking websites for the most up-to-date information on their technical requirements.

Live Video vs. Recorded Video

Your first major decision is whether to broadcast live or post prerecorded video. There are pros and cons to each side!

With recorded video, you can edit, splice, and even rearrange segments to craft a video experience that best communicates your message to accomplish your goal, whether that's educating a prospect about a topic of interest or directly talking to them about signing up for your service. You can remove mistakes and even rerecord parts as needed, as well as add graphics, music, and other elements to tremendously enhance the video. The major drawback is the additional time and money you'll spend editing the content.

Andrew & Pete, whom you met in the foreword of this book, are masters at creating amazingly edited videos that teach *and* entertain. Take a look at their work on their YouTube channel, "Andrew and Pete."

But with live video, you can connect with an audience in real time. You can invite comments and questions and answer them on camera. In fact, that ability can be a huge boon to content creation. Instead of having to come up with material on your own, you can allow your audience to guide you based on their questions.

Of course, live video isn't without challenges. There's a vulnerability to putting yourself on a live feed, not to mention the very real risk of technical glitches. Anything can happen, and whatever does will be seen by your audience. If that doesn't appeal to you, stick to recorded video.

Ultimately, for most brands, live video is the more authentic, powerful, and therefore preferred medium. There's no substitute for the vulnerability and honesty of a live broadcast. You'll find that audience members can learn to connect with, like, and trust you much faster with live video than with recorded ones.

The biggest challenge lies in letting go of the fears that are holding you back. Check out Figure 7–1 below for a quick list of the pros and cons of each.

Either way, it's possible to find tremendous success, so in the next sections we'll outline some tactics with high potential for both live and recorded video content.

LIVE VIDEO	
PROS	**CONS**
You can engage with the audience.	There's more potential for real-time issues.
Audience can inspire content.	Live video can be more frightening.
RECORDED VIDEO	
PROS	**CONS**
Content can be edited and rearranged.	There's no real-time feedback.
It's less frightening.	It's less engaging.

FIGURE 7–1. Pros and cons of live and recorded video

LIVE VIDEO TACTICS

It should go without saying that for any social media tactic to achieve success, it must be replicated, repeated, and structured—in other words, you must have and consistently execute a plan.

This is absolutely essential when it comes to live video.

You cannot broadcast one live video and expect to achieve all your business goals. You must commit to a regular broadcast schedule, such as weekly, that you can promote and build an audience for over time.

Once you determine a frequency for your new "show," you can decide on a format. Will you simply talk to the camera every time? Will you have one or more guests? Will you perform a task, using visual props or featuring products?

Here are some specific ideas for segments or aspects of your live videos:

- Introduction and audience engagement
- Interview guest expert
- Interview customer
- Interview employee
- Demonstrate an app or activity
- Share announcements or product news

Using some of those third-party tools we mentioned earlier, you can host a show and interview or discuss topics of interest with one or more people, creating an educational and entertaining experience for your audience.

The host plus guest(s) format has a lot of benefits. In a typical interview format, you ask questions and the guest responds with their informed experience, making them the primary provider of content for the video. This allows you to create videos on topics that you may know nothing about!

Furthermore, most hosts would agree that having a dialogue with a guest on camera is a lot easier than a monologue. You can ask questions, listen to their answers, add some input of your own, and then ask a follow-up question. And when your guest is an influencer, they could potentially share your video with their own audience and bring in new viewers to your program.

The disadvantage, though, is that in a standard interview format you're limited by the experience and capabilities of your guest. While you can ask any questions you wish, you ultimately have no control over their responses and cannot guarantee they will cover the points you want to hit.

This is where going solo can shine. If it's just you on camera, you can decide in advance exactly what you're going to talk about and which points you want to make. You can have screen shares and examples prepared in advance and ensure that your audience receives exactly what you want them to hear.

Either of these approaches works great—and there's nothing stopping you from using both! Have a mix of dialogues and solo presentations in your live video strategy. Combine interviews with structured talks with open Q&As, and let your audience appreciate the variety and depth with which you cover relevant topics.

RECORDED VIDEO TACTICS

An interesting facet of recorded video is that you can steal many ideas from livestreamers; just prerecord and upload. In fact, with Facebook Premiere, you can publish a recorded video that Facebook will treat like a Live video for the initial broadcast and then as a normal replay/on-demand video thereafter.

You can interview guests, give a solo presentation, and even answer questions from your audience (if they're provided in advance). You can use your smartphone, webcam, or DSLR to record the video. You can even use an app like Ecamm with Skype to bring in a guest and just record it instead of broadcasting live.

The beauty of a recorded video is the wealth of options you have when it comes to video footage. While a livestream is basically limited to whatever camera you have connected at the moment, with the help of some basic editing software, you can pull together almost any recorded footage you can imagine.

Mac users, for instance, can use iMovie to combine multiple video clips, edit and rearrange longer clips, add one or more audio tracks, insert titles and transitions, and export the finished product. PC users can use the free Movie Maker for the same purpose. If you wish to edit your video on mobile, there are iOS and Android apps for that as well, depending on the complexity of your needs.

In fact, you can even combine recorded and live video! YouTube broadcaster Steve Dotto of Dotto Tech quite successfully merges prerecorded demonstrations and screencasts with a live broadcast, giving him the benefit of live interaction and feedback alongside professionally edited footage.

SHORT VS. LONG VIDEOS

Until now, the ideas we've been sharing about video, whether live or recorded, have skewed toward the long side. Generally speaking, if you're going to interview someone or demonstrate something, it'll likely end up lasting 10 to 30 minutes.

And that's good! Facebook in particular has repeatedly said they prefer videos more than ten minutes long, particularly when it comes to live broadcasts—presumably because they are seen as more interesting and informative. And according to Content Career, an online resource for content creators, the average first-page ranking YouTube video is 15 minutes long. So you should always publish long video content, right?

Not so fast.

First, not every question or topic requires a 20-minute discussion. Just like blog posts, the content should be as long as necessary for the topic and audience.

Second, there's definitely a time and a place for short-form content! If you have a weekly show that airs at the same time every week, folks will tune in expecting to sit down and watch for a while. But what about people who just happen to see your posts while browsing Facebook or Twitter? They might not have 20 minutes to spare right then—but perhaps they could watch a two- or three-minute video.

Shorter video content is also far more flexible. It can be used in Stories and even combined with other short videos to tell a wonderful story or explain an interesting topic.

We'll talk more in Chapter 11 about repurposing and reusing social content, particularly video, but keep in mind that a fantastic source of short videos is the longer videos you're already creating! If you broadcast a 30-minute interview with an industry expert, there will definitely be at least a few segments you can clip out and repurpose as shorter videos.

VIDEO GEAR

One of the first reasons people often cite for not creating video content is that it's too expensive to buy the right equipment.

Let us help you with that.

Today, virtually everyone in business has a smartphone, and as we've already covered, you can use that smartphone to livestream or record video anywhere. In fact, under the right conditions, that video footage can be just as good as anything you'd get with a dedicated video camera. Similarly, most laptops come with a built-in webcam and an audio port to plug in a headset and mic.

The biggest drawback to using a laptop or smartphone to record video is that it is harder to compensate for poor lighting. In fact, if you're going to invest in anything for recording video, better lighting should be at the top of your list, particularly if you want to record in a dim office.

When you task a camera to record you in poor light, the resulting video is dark and grainy. Conversely, when you're well-lit, the video is crisp and clear and, most important, your audience can see you nicely.

To that end, the recommended placement of lights is to have two in front of you, on either side of the camera, and one that is directed behind you to eliminate shadows. You'll find that lights designed specifically for video work can be adjusted and directed more easily than normal household lights, but feel free to work with what you have.

To test your lighting, simply open a video recording program on your computer, such as QuickTime for macOS, and see how your video quality looks. Are you grainy or shadowed? Lit too harshly? Get up and move your lights accordingly and then see how that impacted the quality of the video. If necessary, record yourself briefly and send it to a friend for input.

You can test your audio quality the same way. Record an audio-only segment of you speaking and play it back to hear how you sound. If you're too faint, try positioning the microphone closer to your mouth when you talk.

This is where choosing to use a smartphone over a laptop can actually be an advantage. If you simply *go outside* on a nice day, prop up your phone, and hit record, you can create *amazing* video content! Plus you may have the added benefit of interesting scenery to use as your background.

Andrew Davis is an accomplished content marketing genius and worldwide speaker. If he only recorded video in a polished studio, he'd seldom publish due to his packed travel schedule. Instead, he records wherever he is—sometimes with his phone and other times with a DSLR—and always in interesting places like Boston, Prague, or the nearest beach.

The key with video content is to focus on getting the tech to the point where you can create nicely lit, beautifully mic'd video, and then shift your focus to the content. Investing in equipment for your video content should be a choice to make it easier or more flexible when it comes to creating that content. Not a requirement.

And the good news is, even if you do decide to buy some equipment, the cost isn't prohibitive and can be spread out over time. For instance, you might want to consider:

- *External Webcam*. While a built-in webcam is convenient, most are quite basic and will struggle in poor lighting. Logitech is the industry standard for external webcams.
- *External Microphone*. You should never use the built-in microphone to record video, particularly if you are livestreaming. Earbuds are OK, but if you want great sound, invest in a USB microphone such as the Blue Yeti or Audio-Technica's ATR2100.
- *DSLR Camera*. A DSLR camera combines the mechanism of a single lens with digital imaging, allowing you to take thousands of amazing pictures and shoot gorgeous video! DSLR cameras can be used for both recorded and live video and are a smart investment.
- *Lighting, Lighting, Lighting*. We can't stress enough the importance of good lighting. Film yourself and be critical of the lighting. Look at other people's videos and see how well they're lit. You'll probably need to turn on and bring in far more lights than you think you'll need. But it's worth it!

VIDEO BEST PRACTICES

A few final thoughts and tips on video content before we start geeking out on chatbots and automation.

We mentioned before how effective eye contact is for establishing a connection with your audience. It's how you start building rapport. People who *never look* at the camera risk suggesting to the audience that they cannot be trusted.

That's not to say you can't take your eyes off the camera. But the more you can directly look at the camera—making each and every viewer feel like you're looking at them—the more effective your videos will be.

So practice that! Get into the habit of looking at the camera while you're speaking. Treat it as though it's the person you're talking to—if it helps, imagine it's a dear friend you're having a wonderful conversation with.

One trick is to minimize whatever video screen you're looking at. Make it small and centered at the top of your monitor, so it's as close to your camera as possible. That way, even if you're looking at yourself, other guests, or a feed of comments from a live screen, your eyes are never far from the camera.

It's also important to give yourself time and grace when it comes to creating video content. No one is born knowing how to produce gorgeous videos. It takes many, many hours of practice and experience to get good at it, and even then, like every other skill, it takes a lifetime to master it.

Remember that generally speaking, your audience and viewers are rooting for you! They want to learn from you and connect with you, and they will bear with you as you struggle here or there.

If you're broadcasting live and say something wrong, just laugh it off and move on. Heck, some of the video clips that have gone the most viral for the 360 Marketing Squad are the blooper reels Stephanie inevitably pulls out. Those actually serve a wonderful purpose: They show your authenticity, humanity, and hopefully your sense of humor!

Finally, when you're deciding on your video strategy—where you're publishing videos and what you're going to talk about—also include a time frame for how long you're going to commit to doing this before you render any real judgment.

It can be discouraging to spend hours filming and editing a video only to publish it and get no views. But don't let that stop you! Publish the next one, and the next one, and the one after that. Keep pushing out that content and scratching out an audience for yourself. If you're not sure whether the videos are good, find trusted friends and colleagues who can give you candid, professional feedback, and then keep publishing the videos.

It takes a long time to build an audience and even longer to start incorporating feedback and input and get great at making videos. Give yourself sufficient time to accomplish that, and have some reasonable expectations and metrics as a gauge for success.

Chapter 8

Leverage Chatbots and Automation

Chatbots are an extremely effective way for businesses to scale engagement and nurture social communities into real business results, and this chapter provides an outstanding overview.

Let's look at an example. Becky runs a fun boutique cupcake shop in Cleveland, Ohio. She sells ginormous cupcakes in her downtown location, caters birthday parties, and helps keep Cuyahoga County's sugar levels at maximum capacity.

Like most bakeries, Becky's operation is lean. When she's not running the counter and checking on customers, she's in the back mixing and baking and icing gigantic baked goods. After hours, she takes care of her books and marketing and vendor relationships.

You know what she doesn't have time to do? Check Messenger on her phone multiple times a day to answer questions. She knows how important it is to respond to customers and engage with her audience, particularly when they're asking things like, "How late are you open?" and "How much for a dozen cupcakes?" But realistically, she's too busy minding the store to be mindful of messages.

Fortunately, she doesn't have to.

Becky worked with a chatbot consultant to create *Bot Becky*—a programmed chatbot that will automatically answer many of the common questions and messages on her bakery's Facebook Page. She can even use the bot to run specials and contests and keep her growing community of fans informed and engaged.

How did she do it? What exactly is a chatbot, anyway? And do you really have to name it? We'll answer all those questions and more in this chapter.

CHATBOTS DEFINED

It's important to know what chatbots are and are not if you're going to use their wonderful capabilities in your own business.

- Chatbots *are not* artificial intelligence—they don't learn and adapt and definitely do not have plans for global domination.
- Chatbots *are* programmable and customizable. The questions they can answer and the resources they can deliver are limited only by your imagination.
- Chatbots *are not* a free way to spam your followers. You must employ a tool to manage subscribers, messages, and work flows, and there are strict limitations on how much you can broadcast messages.
- Chatbots *are* a way to automatically scale the capability of your business to address customer questions and engage your audience.

A chatbot is simply a piece of software that can carry on a conversation—a chat—whether digital or audio, with some degree of automation. If you've ever called in to a large company and had a "conversation" with an automated system where you answered its questions verbally, you were talking to a chatbot.

But that's not quite the kind of chatbot we're talking about in this chapter. Instead, we're dealing exclusively with Messenger bots—chatbots that are programmed specifically to work with Facebook Messenger in conjunction with your business's Facebook Page.

Instagram and WhatsApp, as Facebook-owned social platforms, also support chatbot automation, though only rudimentary at present, and providers are beginning to emerge for networks like YouTube and Twitch. We believe that over the next five years, most other platforms will follow suit, making such capability as ubiquitous as live video.

Because of the broad presence of Facebook, acceptance of Messenger automation, and ease of use, we will focus on Messenger bots whenever we cite specific capabilities or implementation steps. If you're interested in implementing automation on an alternate platform, virtually all the same concepts will apply when that platform adopts chatbots.

At a basic level, a chatbot is a programmed assistant that can perform certain tasks and respond to certain inquiries. But it's actually much, much more than that.

Within your existing Facebook Page, you actually have basic chatbot capability! If you go to your on desktop and then click the Automated Responses tab, you can set up limited automated responses to specific questions or messages followers may send you. Options include:

- *Away messages.* Manually schedule times you are unavailable or allow Facebook to automatically detect when you are away and send a reply to the user to let them know how long you will be away and when you will respond.

- *Instant reply.* Make a good first impression. Send a custom message instantly to someone the first time they message your Facebook Page or Instagram profile. If you also have away messages turned on, they will receive your away message instead.

- *Location and contact information.* Allow Facebook to detect when a user is messaging your Page to inquire about your location or contact information and customize an automatic response.

- *Frequently asked questions.* Suggest up to four questions that people can ask your Page with simple, automated responses for each question. Add these at the beginning of a conversation with your Page, or attach it to a menu that people can access at any time when sending messages to your Page. A menu can have up to five options.

- *Page recommend.* Ten minutes after someone publicly recommends your Page (the equivalent to Google's 5-star reviews), Facebook can send the user an automated thank-you from your Page, as you can see in Figure 8–1 on page 112.

- *Page not recommend.* This is your chance to automatically follow up with a user ten minutes after they choose not to recommend your Page, which allows you to address concerns and provide prompt customer service. You can even include a button that links to an offer or special opportunity, or add a video message to your reply. Imagine receiving a 30-second video message from the head of a company, thanking you for your feedback and acknowledging that your concerns are being addressed. This feature is especially good for Page owners with limited manpower for responding to messages and feedback.

- *Application received.* Are you posting job openings on Facebook? When someone responds to your job post, automatically send the applicant a reply message to acknowledge receipt and set expectations for the follow-up they will receive.

- *Reminders.* If you are using Facebook's Appointments feature, which allows users to schedule a meeting with you, you can automatically send a reminder message the day before.

- *Follow-up messages.* After an appointment, send a message to the user with a reminder to encourage their next step or suggest that they book another meeting.

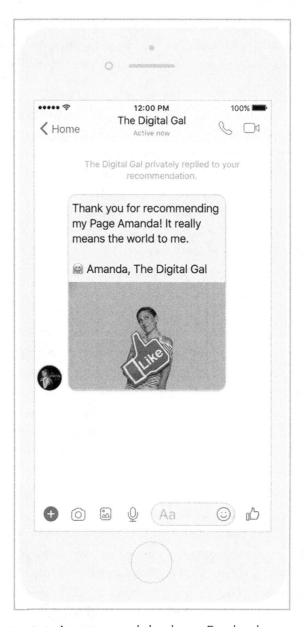

FIGURE 8–1. An automated thank-you Facebook message

Becky can use Facebook's built in messenger tools to set up an away message to respond outside business hours, automatically reply to a customer inquiring about hours and directions to her shop, provide an answer to a frequently asked question about flavors and pricing, schedule appointments for order pickup, and send a follow-up message asking for feedback on an order of cupcakes. As a business owner, this can save Becky valuable time while providing her clientele with an elevated level of customer service.

As you can see, Facebook's platform has some very useful built-in options that allow you to customize your messages and automate portions of the user experience. However, these options are heavily templated. That makes Facebook's built-in Messenger options very useful for the novice who is just getting started with chatbot automation, but it can seem limited when we compare it with the power of using third-party software to create and manage your Messenger chatbot conversations.

By using software such as ManyChat, MobileMonkey, or HubSpot's Chatbot Builder to create your Messenger chatbot, you can set up a more robust series of responses based on how the user engages with your chatbot. Think of it like a "choose your own adventure" book where users are in control of the conversation: They can discover what information they need next.

Now when one of Becky's potential new customers sends a message to her Facebook Page, they can choose to browse images of Cuyahoga County's most requested cupcakes, then navigate to pricing options for a dozen enormous signature cupcakes for delivery vs. a batch of mini custom red velvet cupcakes for pickup. If they are still interested, they can browse links to Becky's top cupcake recipe on Pinterest, check out her "Bakery Business Boss" tips on LinkedIn, or watch her latest Facebook Live video, a behind-the-scenes look at getting a 12-tier cupcake cake ready for the biggest socialite wedding Cuyahoga County has ever seen. All this is available without leaving Messenger. If the customer has questions while browsing through options and content, they can request a live chat with Becky at any time, and she will receive a notification to enter a chat in Messenger.

How does all this benefit Becky's business? It is capturing the potential customer's attention and curiosity and getting them to *engage* with her business and social profiles when they are ready and have the time, independent of business hours. Engagement and attention span are our online currency; they lead to awareness, relationship building, trust, and ultimately sales. Becky is also positioning herself to have an open line of communication with this potential customer; she can give them instant answers so they don't have to leave the platform and search for information elsewhere.

How many people are comfortable chatting with a stranger over text? Not too many. How many are comfortable chatting with "a business" on Messenger? A surprising number.

In addition to elevating the user experience, you can incorporate ways to automate tasks to reduce the amount of administrative work. For example, Becky can collect a customer's cupcake order, get their contact information, and take payment, all through her Messenger chatbot. She can automatically have her customer's information pushed into her CRM (customer relationship management) system, add their email to her email marketing list, add them to her Facebook Custom Audience (a targeting option for Facebook ads that we'll cover in Chapter 9) for future online marketing including specials, and so much more.

Are you getting excited about Messenger chatbots yet? Let's take it one step further.

Becky is attending a wedding convention in San Diego. Typically this is her biggest networking event of the year, where she connects with other bakers, florists, and industry experts who help her boost her cupcake creativity and bring new ideas back to her cupcake shop. In past years, Becky has come home exhausted with a handful of business cards, too tired to go through each card and remember who they were or why they were going to connect. This year, she is leveraging the power of her Messenger bot to stay organized and efficient.

Instead of exchanging business cards when she meets someone she wants to connect with, Becky has a QR code saved on the lock screen of her phone that links to a special Messenger chatbot she set up before the convention. She can ask the other person to scan her code with their phone camera, which will open Facebook Messenger on their phone (assuming they have it installed; 1.3 billion people use it every month, so the odds are pretty good) and launch into a "business card" conversation with all of Becky's contact information and links to her social profiles. The chatbot then asks them for their email address and a one-sentence reminder on what they talked to Becky about.

When they answer, the bot automatically pushes their name, email, and talking points into a Google spreadsheet. When Becky returns home from the convention, she will have a spreadsheet of contacts ready for her to follow up on, along with reminder notes on what they talked about and links to their Facebook profiles.

If building a Messenger chatbot seems intimidating, think of it like a pile of Lego blocks. When you got a new Lego set when you were little, at first you followed the instructions to assemble

>
>
> **TIP**
>
> Facebook also has a built-in QR code scanner. Type "QR code scanner" in Facebook's search bar on mobile and voilà! You can scan QR codes. This is a handy trick if the user's phone camera cannot scan the codes.

the blocks just as they looked in the pictures. When you outgrew that task, then you started to get creative and assemble the blocks using your imagination to build whatever you wanted.

Building a chatbot is similar. Each component, such as bringing in an image or a text block, is like a Lego block. Some of the components you can use include:

- Text block
- Image

- Card (image, headline, description, and button)
- Gallery (up to ten cards you can swipe/scroll back and forth)
- Audio clip
- Video clip
- File (such as a PDF document)

The possibilities are endless, and you are limited only by your own creativity when it comes to how you want to assemble your components to present the conversation. Focus on keeping your conversation flows curious, interesting, and focused on the subscriber.

We have talked about what a Messenger chatbot can do for you on the customer-facing side, but what does that look like behind the scenes?

Subscribers

When a user sends a message for the first time to your Page with a third-party chatbot connected, they automatically become a *subscriber* to your Messenger chatbot. This may seem comparable to adding a new subscriber to your email marketing list, but chatbot subscribers are nothing like email subscribers and should be marketed to quite differently. Facebook has certain rules and requirements that we must follow in order to use Messenger chatbots.

24-Hour Rule

After someone sends a message to your Page and becomes a subscriber, you have up to 24 hours to respond. The 24-hour rule is required by Facebook no matter which third-party chatbot tool you are using; it is designed to reduce spam or unwanted messages. Within 24 hours of interaction, you can reply to one-on-one messages or send a *broadcast message* to subscribers, which is a message sent to multiple subscribers at once. This can include promotional messages. After that 24-hour window closes, you cannot send messages to that person until they initiate conversation again, unless it is related to a customer-service issue in a live chat; in that case the messages cannot be promotional. There are some exceptions to the 24-hour rule, including:

- Confirmed event update
- Post-purchase update
- Account update
- Human agent (that is, a response from a human being and not a chatbot)

If your message falls into one of these categories, you can send it past the 24-hour limit. The consequences of sending a message in breach of the 24-hour rule include having your Page's messaging abilities restricted or having your Page shut down.

One way in which your Messenger chatbot subscribers do resemble an email mailing list is in your ability to segment or "tag" your lists. You can add tags to subscribers to categorize them in any way you wish. For example, Becky may tag all subscribers who submit an order, and apply a different tag to subscribers who wanted a price quote on red velvet cupcakes compared with chocolate. That way, the next time she runs a flash sale on red velvet cupcakes for new customers, she can create a list of subscribers who have not yet bought from her and who have previously asked about the price for red velvet cupcakes.

Armed with that knowledge, let's get you started with your first chatbot.

HOW TO START YOUR FIRST CHATBOT

In order to use Messenger marketing to its fullest capacity, you are going to need third-party software, unless you have the coding skills to create one on your own. There are dozens of easy-to-use, third-party options with varying feature sets and prices, such as MobileMonkey, Chatfuel, Botsify, or HubSpot's Chatbot Builder. We typically recommend and use ManyChat for its affordable pricing, broad capability, and quick learning curve. For those reasons we will use their platform as the basis for the following section, but most of these concepts will apply to whatever tool you decide to use.

Set Up ManyChat

Let's walk through the basic steps of setting up ManyChat:

1. Go to their website and click on Get Started Free to start creating your new account. You will be able to open an account and do everything outlined below to start your first chatbot completely free!

2. Sign in using your Facebook account and then select which Facebook Page you would like to set up a chatbot for. If you aren't already an admin for the Page you want to work with, obtain that access from the Page owner first.

3. Once you choose your Facebook Page, ManyChat will ask for permission to do a series of tasks, such as Manage Your Page. Unless you have a specific business reason not to use a chatbot for something in particular, you can safely leave all permissions activated and complete the signup process.

4. Give ManyChat a little background about your business and needs so it can tailor the experience for you, click Connect for the Page you want to manage, and proceed to the Dashboard.

You have now successfully connected your Messenger chatbot! This is where the fun begins.

There are some things you should note right away. Once you connect a Messenger chatbot, people messaging your Page for the first time will now see a "Get Started" button that they must click on in Messenger to be able to send your Page a message. By clicking "Get Started," they automatically become a subscriber.

By default, a user can type "Stop" or "Unsubscribe" at any time to unsubscribe from your bot. Because most people are unaware of this, it is good practice to include this information in your first interaction with a new subscriber. You can do this while setting up your welcome message, which we will address a little later in this chapter.

Navigating Around ManyChat

When you log in to ManyChat, you can navigate among the following sections:

- Dashboard
- Audience
- Live Chat
- Growth Tools
- Broadcasting
- Automation
- Flows
- Settings
- Templates
- My Account

The Dashboard is where you can see, at a glance, how your subscriber growth is progressing. Like any platform, your number of subscribers shouldn't be a goal or a vanity metric, but expanding your audience *is* important. Not only is this how you can see how successful your efforts have been, but if you do any specific campaigns for attracting subscribers this is an easy way to see how those campaigns performed as well.

The Dashboard is also where you will find your Bot Link. This is a link that will immediately open Messenger for whoever clicks on it and allow them to begin to interact with your bot, as you can see in Figure 8–2 on page 118.

Consider for a moment when you might want to give someone a link that they can click to follow you, receive a free resource, learn more, subscribe to your newsletter, join your group, buy a course . . . or *all of the above!* In many ways, chatbot options are limited only by your time and imagination.

ManyChat's Audience tab is used to view your subscribers and sort them by tags you have assigned, by the widgets they interacted with, by sequences they are subscribed to, or by Facebook ads they were sent from. Here you can inspect individual subscribers

FIGURE 8–2. Bot link

and/or do bulk actions to manage your subscriber lists such as changing tags or adding new ones.

The Live Chat tab allows you to view and respond to incoming messages. This can be especially helpful if you have a high volume of automatic messages but don't want to lose track of other messages being sent to your Page. Without the Live Chat feature, they can easily get lost in your Messenger inbox.

Use the Broadcasting tab to send broadcasted messages to all or segments of your audience who have engaged with your Messenger chatbot in the past 24 hours or to those who meet one of the category exceptions: confirmed event update, post-purchase update, or account update.

One of the first questions after you set up your chatbot is how to get subscribers. This is where Growth Tools comes in. Growth Tools include *widgets* and *ads*. Let's explore the widgets first:

- *Overlay Widgets.* Small overlays that can appear on your website as a pop-up window, a full screen takeover, an opt-in bar at the top of the website, or an opt-in window that slides in from the side. Each overlay widget has individual options that you can tailor to match the appearance of your website.
- *Embeddable Widgets.* An opt-in box or a button that can be embedded anywhere in your website.

- *Landing Page.* A simple web page where you can encourage people to opt in to your bot.
- *Messenger Ref URL.* URL links that can send people into specific bot flows or conversations.
- *Facebook Ads JSON.** A snippet of code that you can embed into your Facebook ads. This would be considered a more advanced feature.
- *Facebook Comments.* A feature in which your Messenger bot can send an opt-in message to anyone who comments on a chosen post on your Facebook Page—or anyone who comments with a specific keyword. This feature has been less reliable and sometimes works inconsistently, but it is by far one of the most engaging growth tools to get people to interact with your bot.
- *QR Code.* A scannable QR code that launches the user into the bot flow or conversation of your choice.
- *Customer Chat.* A chat window you can embed on your website to chat with your visitors.
- *Checkbox.** A checkbox you can include on your website to allow people to become a subscriber.

*Paid features that require a ManyChat Pro subscription, typically starting at $10/month.

The Automation tab allows you to set up a wide range of automatic actions that take place based on how a user interacts with your bot. This section includes:

- *Main Menu.* A navigation option that remains anchored and visible on Messenger on mobile devices. This menu is commonly used to promote a call to action, such as setting up an appointment or visiting your website.
- *Default Reply.* A message that is sent to a user when the bot doesn't know how to reply. Think of this as a safety net, used when the bot gets confused or doesn't have the next answer programmed in.
- *Welcome Message.* The message a subscriber sees the first time they enter your chatbot directly from messaging your Facebook Page. The welcome message is a good place to tell subscribers:
  - That they are receiving messages from a bot, not a real human
  - How they can request a live human to enter the conversation

> **TIP**
>
> In addition to the growth tools listed above, one of the most powerful ways to get people to engage with your bot is to connect it to your Facebook and Instagram ads. This can be done when creating your ads with Facebook Ads Manager. (We'll discuss Ads Manager more in Chapter 9.)

- That they can unsubscribe at any time by typing "stop" or "unsubscribe." (These keywords are built into ManyChat and will initiate the unsubscribe function.)
- The welcome message is also a great opportunity to establish your brand voice or your bot's personality. Some regions, such as California, have laws to prevent bots from being passed off as real people. To avoid confusion, many businesses have adopted a brand personality or "mascot persona" for their bot. For instance, to promote their TV show *Genius*, National Geographic adopted the personality of Einstein for their bot.

- *Keywords.* Automated replies to a subscriber based on the keyword they type.
- *Sequences.* A series of messages sent automatically to a subscriber, similar to an email marketing drip campaign.
- *Rules.* Automatic events that you can program to occur based on actions a subscriber takes when interacting with your bot.
- *Pixel.* A small snippet of code that you can install on your website to trigger data to push into ManyChat based on events on your website.

The Flows tab is where you organize all your flows or conversations. These are what you use to build your different Messenger chatbot conversations that people will interact with. For example, you can build one flow or conversation for your frequently asked questions. You can set up another to register subscribers to your program, and a third to deliver a free PDF download.

Go to the Settings tab to manage users, billing, your time zone, notifications, and an entire range of options. This is also where you will set up your greeting text—the small paragraph of text that people will see in Messenger before they hit the Get Started button.

It is best practice to set up your greeting text to encourage visitors to click the Get Started button. You can even personalize it with the user's name to make your Messenger interaction a friendly and inviting experience, as you can see in Figure 8–3 on page 121.

The Templates section allows you to browse bot templates that you can install and revise to suit your needs. You can also create your own Messenger chatbot templates that you can share with other ManyChat accounts. You can protect your templates when sharing them by using a one-time use link. You can also lock the flows within a template to prevent editing once they are installed by another account.

The My Account section is where you can access Agency features, either to become a certified ManyChat Agency Partner or Messenger Marketing Expert, or to manage your profile for your account.

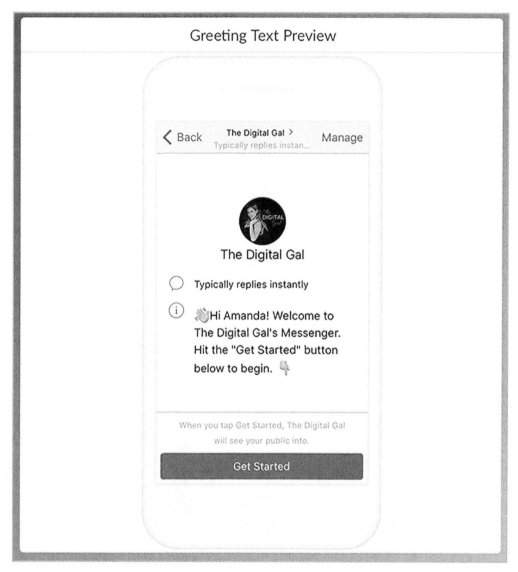

FIGURE 8–3. Sample greeting text

With this overview of ManyChat, you will be able to get started with that tool or any of the similar third-party Messenger Marketing tools easily!

Owning a small business comes with a lot of responsibility and very little extra time. Becky's Messenger chatbot can save her hours each week while allowing her to provide an excellent level of customer service. This helps her stay ahead of her competition and buys back some precious time to spend with her family as she grows her business efficiently.

Chapter 9

Leverage Paid Social Media

The best way to rapidly grow an online audience, and keep your brand top of mind and tip of tongue, is through paid advertising. In this chapter, you will learn which social media networks support advertising and how to handle creating your first campaign.

Between your website, hosting, and a few other tools (like Easil or Agorapulse), if you haven't yet dipped your toe into online advertising, you're probably spending $100 or less per month on marketing. Assuming you're willing to create content and manage your social media yourself, you should be able to invest some money into paid advertising.

While there are many options, like banner ads, Fiverr campaigns, and so on, in our experience, you'll get the best return with Google Ads and Facebook Ads. Depending on your business and target audience, you might also consider ads on Twitter, Pinterest, and/or LinkedIn. Those three tend to have a higher *cost per click* (CPC), however, so let's focus on Google and Facebook initially. (We'll explain why we're including non-social advertising with Google in a moment.)

GOOGLE ADS

When you decide to advertise with Google, you have a lot of options, but we'll give you a high-level perspective here so you can decide if it's interesting to you.

Using Google Ads, you can place advertisements above or near search results that are relevant to your business and brand. Because the audience is people who are actively searching on a particular topic or keyword, we refer to this as *search intent*. You don't have to guess whether they're interested in that topic—they are.

Additionally, Google serves ads on actual websites, so you can place your ads in its "Display Network" and reach people who are, perhaps, reading about a topic but not necessarily searching for it on Google. The sites in the Display Network have signed up for Google's AdSense program; they earn a commission for every ad view and click.

When you place ads with Google, you set a bid amount and a daily budget. The *bid amount* is the maximum amount you're willing to spend per click (e.g., 25 cents), and your ad then competes against other advertisers interested in reaching the same audience. Ads with higher bids are displayed first on each page of search results, or more often on content sites within the display network.

Again, you're only charged when someone clicks on your ad, so you'll want to find a balance between ranking high for your ad and getting enough clicks, leads, and sales to make it worthwhile.

Your ads will continue to display until you reach your daily budget limit and then stop automatically, so it's up to you how much you spend.

FACEBOOK ADS

When you decide to advertise with Facebook, you can either create a new ad or use a status update you've already shared.

The ad fee structure is similar to Google in that you can set a daily budget, but you don't set a bid per click. Instead, Facebook will begin showing your ads; the more interest people show, the less per click you'll be charged. So it's in everyone's best interests to create Facebook ad posts that are interesting and compelling.

In addition to driving traffic, you can use Facebook ads for brand awareness and simply pay for *engagement*—in other words, likes, comments, and shares. The more people engage with your ad and post, the more likely it is to be seen by people outside your target audience.

Unlike Google search ads, which are 100 percent text, Facebook ads can be links, images, or even video. You can use a single image or a carousel of images. You can even upload multiple images and let Facebook test which one resonates best with your audience.

You can also set up a *remarketing pixel* (a snippet of code installed on your website) so that Facebook can track users who have been to your site and allow you to "remarket" to them with an ad specifically targeting them. Let's explore this concept further.

THE POWER OF SEARCH + REMARKETING

Here's how remarketing works. Once you have a Facebook pixel installed on your site and are driving targeted traffic using Google Ads (and, of course, other means), you are equipped to amplify the frequency illusion we talked about in Chapter 7.

With a pixel in place, you can now create Facebook ads targeting people who have visited your site, or even specific pages or posts within your site. This is referred to as retargeting or remarketing.

You've doubtless experienced this yourself. Spend a couple of minutes looking at cars on Infiniti.com, and suddenly every site you go to is displaying Infiniti ads. Because you showed interest in a brand or product by visiting their site, advertisers smartly wish to capitalize on that interest and keep themselves top of mind.

You can now do exactly the same thing!

When your Google ads effectively capture someone as they're searching for you or information you have published, they register as a visitor with the Facebook pixel. If Facebook recognizes them as a user *and* you are running a remarketing campaign that includes someone like them, you can layer brand-awareness or added-benefit advertising on Facebook or Instagram, which will potentially be seen by someone who was already demonstrating search intent *and* is familiar with your brand. This is extraordinarily powerful and effective.

Couple this technique with problem-solving content, and you now have a means to reach people who you know have an issue and may need help to solve it. That help might include:

- How-to guides
- Answers to frequently asked questions
- Case studies

Let's say you're a local attorney specializing in family law. You can write a series of blog posts that answer common questions about divorce, child custody, estate planning, and so on, and then use Google Ads to help people who are searching for those answers find your content. You can then place Facebook ads that encourage those people to call you for more information and assistance.

Or let's imagine you own a wedding dress shop. Same scenario: Create content that answers common questions brides have about their special day, use Google Ads to drive intentional traffic, and then leverage Facebook to make sure those brides know about your gorgeous dresses by placing ads showcasing your latest offerings and retargeting your website traffic.

Whatever products or services you have to offer, this technique can be implemented, tested, refined, and then scaled up.

OTHER PLATFORMS

As we mentioned earlier, Facebook isn't the only option when it comes to social advertising. It's worth taking a moment to consider and even test each of the other networks, particularly if that platform and predominant audience suit your business.

Instagram

You may already know that since Instagram is owned by Facebook, advertising on Instagram is handled within the Facebook Ads Manager. Ads are similarly structured, and campaigns that you launch on Facebook can also include Instagram.

So why didn't we just include Instagram in the previous section?

First, it is a separate platform, which means your audience and results will be very different from Facebook. The demographics of Instagram users tend to skew younger than Facebook's, for instance.

Second, Instagram's aesthetic is one of square images and video, with short captions and hashtags. While it's possible for Facebook advertising assets to look good on Instagram, it's more likely that you will need to revise your ads before they run there.

When crafting an ad campaign in Facebook Ads Manager, you build the ad and select your destinations. You can then preview how the ad will look on Facebook vs. Instagram, mobile vs. desktop, and so on. Always check those previews, and if the ad does not render beautifully on all platforms, take a moment to create a separate campaign with alternative assets.

Third, realize that people on Instagram do not expect to click on outside links. Since standard image and video posts cannot have working links, people are accustomed to simply scrolling through their Instagram feeds. Ads, however, can include links, which appear as a Learn More bar across the bottom of the ad.

So an ad link that might get a decent clickthrough rate on Facebook may not perform as well on Instagram. Consider carefully what you hope to achieve with the Instagram ad, and choose the imagery and copy you need to elicit that behavior. While organic referral traffic from Instagram is still poor, ad-driven and ecommerce referral traffic is increasing exponentially for that network.

At the end of the day, realize that Instagram will likely be your poorest driver of traffic. Granted, anyone who does tap on an Instagram-promoted link is likely very interested in learning more about what you're promoting. But most people will just keep scrolling.

Twitter

There are several different kinds of ads you can run on Twitter, each with different benefits and mechanisms.

First, just like Facebook and Instagram, you can choose to create an ad from scratch within the advertising dashboard, or you can promote an existing tweet. In fact, when creating a campaign in Twitter, you can choose to include multiple tweets within that campaign.

Suppose you have published an ebook and have already posted several tweets about it, each including a link to a landing page that offers it to new subscribers. You could bundle all those tweets into a campaign that promotes and amplifies each tweet accordingly.

One significant difference in terms of ad placement is that Twitter gives you the option of promoting a tweet into someone's feed depending on who they are, who they're following, or what they're searching on. Let's break that down.

Because Twitter doesn't use extensive research about sections, nor does it have pages to follow or groups to join, the amount of personal information it can collect about its users is quite minimal. Therefore, while there are some limited targeting options, such as basic demographics and interests, that's not what Twitter wants you to focus on.

Instead, you would target your followers, followers of other accounts, and look-alike audiences based on those other accounts. Obviously, it helps at this point to have a good understanding of your industry and the top Twitter profiles your target audience may be interested in.

This might include competitors, educational organizations, and sources of industry news.

The assumption is that because someone is following X, they must therefore be interested in Y, and may possibly click to learn more about Z. If this sounds tricky and unreliable, that's because it is.

A more effective form of targeting hearkens back to how we approached Google: search intent. But what do people search for on Twitter? Hashtags and keywords.

When crafting your promotional campaign, you can choose to target specific keywords or keyword phrases, and when your audience searches for those, your promoted tweet will appear at the top of the results. Neat, huh?

What's notable about Twitter campaigns is that you can combine follower targeting and keyword targeting for a really interesting mix of opportunities to get your tweet content in front of your desired audience.

You can, of course, promote your profile if you'd like to use ad dollars to reach and grow your audience. You can even allow Twitter to automatically promote your channel's content, a service that has been dubbed "Twitter Promote Mode." The platform says, "On average, accounts will reach 30,000 additional people and add 30 followers each month." It costs a flat $99 per month and isn't a bad idea for new or relatively new accounts.

LinkedIn

For years, LinkedIn has been relatively ignored by marketers and advertisers due to the limiting belief that it was only for professionals seeking employment and networking.

All that is true, of course, but LinkedIn is so much more than that today.

With the addition of LinkedIn Live video, users can connect in a far more relatable way. It has also become a very viable publishing platform, resulting in higher *and* longer usage—both elements of user behavior that are essential to successful advertising.

What's unique about LinkedIn is the high degree of targeting granularity you can achieve. Consider job titles, for instance. On Facebook, users may or may not enter their job title or keep it updated as their role changes. On LinkedIn, however, most will make sure that and other key elements of their profile are up-to-date and complete.

This means if you want to target CMOs with your advertising because you have a marketing automation tool they might be interested in, you can easily find them on LinkedIn.

Most other elements of advertising on LinkedIn are similar to other platforms. You create campaigns and campaign groups and ads within those to maintain structure and organization. The ads themselves can be images or videos with links, and they can be limited and targeted to specific locations or other demographics.

One important note: Advertising on LinkedIn is still the most expensive of all social media platforms. You can expect to spend several dollars per click on average, and therefore the minimum daily budget for any campaign is $10. However, if you're able to place lucrative offers in front of a highly segmented and interested audience, you have a high likelihood of success.

Pinterest

Pinterest advertising is currently segmented into six types of campaigns:

1. Awareness
2. Traffic
3. App install
4. Shopping
5. Conversions
6. Video views

Most of these are similar to the ads on other social media platforms like Facebook. Using ads to build awareness or drive traffic makes sense. It's interesting that Pinterest has separate campaigns for app installs and video views. But shopping and conversions campaigns are where Pinterest can be of real benefit.

Shopping, of course, has to do with product sales, so if you're selling items through your website this is a very viable campaign objective.

When Pinterest says "conversions," they're specifically referring to nonpurchase conversions such as subscriptions or downloads.

The beauty of having these varied campaign objectives to choose from is that any campaign you set up will be optimized to achieve that objective. And that means the cost of the campaign will be optimized as well. While ads on other platforms can drive traffic to a product, and can even measure the resulting conversions, they're less able to algorithmically benefit from those sales and generate more.

When creating Pinterest campaigns, you should install the Pinterest pixel on your site (just like on Facebook, Twitter, and LinkedIn). Not only will that allow you to measure the results of your ads post-click, but it will also help you target website visitors through remarketing, as we discussed earlier.

As you start to create your campaign, you will see a variety of initial audiences to add, including:

- Engaged pinners (people who have engaged with your Pinterest pins)
- Lookalike pinners (a larger audience based on your own pinners)
- Website visitors

Depending on the type of campaign you select, you will have more options to select from next, such as Product Category, Interests, or Keywords.

With Interests, unfortunately, you're restricted to Pinterest's somewhat limited set, which is based on what typical Pinterest users are pinning. These categories may have nothing to do with your business, but they include:

- Animals
- Architecture
- Art
- Beauty
- Children's fashion
- Design
- DIY and crafts
- Education
- Electronics
- Entertainment
- Event planning
- Finance
- Food and drinks
- Gardening

- Health
- Home decor
- Men's fashion
- Parenting
- Quotes
- Sport
- Travel
- Vehicles
- Wedding
- Women's fashion

If you aren't a heavy Pinterest user yourself, this list (each of which has several subcategories to choose from) should be very telling. Pinterest generally attracts people who are planning or dreaming, so whether it's recipes, clothes, travel destinations, or home improvement projects, that's how most people search and use Pinterest. If your business or pin content falls within one of those interests, drill down and select the most appropriate category. If not, skip that section.

Keywords, on the other hand, are where any brand can leverage user behavior, history, and, most important, intent. Just like with Twitter, you can target keywords on Pinterest and capture user intent when they're actually searching for the information or solution you offer. And Pinterest makes this exceedingly easy.

In the Keyword area of campaign creation, type in a short keyword or phrase to the right, and below that Pinterest will automatically populate it with actual searches by users, as well the search volume. You can then choose from suggested keywords and make sure there's adequate monthly volume to make advertising worthwhile.

As you add keywords, they'll appear in your growing list to the left. Pinterest recommends a minimum of 25 keywords to target, so keep plugging in ideas and selecting recommendations until you have at least that many.

There are minimal demographic options to select, such as gender or age, and unfortunately you can only advertise within the United States.

You may select a daily or lifetime budget, and then either create new pins or choose from existing pins to promote. Once you've done that, you're ready to launch your first campaign!

YouTube

As you know, YouTube is all about videos, so unsurprisingly, ads must be in video format as well. You must upload the video you choose for your ad to your YouTube channel, but it can be private or unlisted if you do not wish for people to view it organically.

YouTube ads can run at the beginning of other people's videos (pre-roll) or during their videos (in-stream). The videos on which your ads play are determined either by topic or channel, along with standard demographic filters that you choose when creating the ad. You can select very specific criteria, such as a particular channel, or choose broad criteria and allow YouTube's algorithm to place your ad accordingly.

YouTube, which is owned by Google, uses Google Ads to manage ad campaigns and preferences. So if you've run Google ads in the past, a lot about YouTube advertising will seem familiar. But unlike Google ads, which are charged per click, YouTube ads are charged per view.

And they are extremely affordable! Brands can leverage YouTube ads to generate thousands of ad views for as little as $1 a day.

But keep in mind, viewers can skip most ads after a few seconds, and even if they watch the entire ad, they are unlikely to take immediate action. YouTube ads are best used for brand awareness, similar to TV commercials.

A lot will depend on your brand, what you're advertising, and the videos on which that ad appears. Try to imagine your viewer's frame of mind—is it likely they will see your ad and be willing to tap to learn more immediately? If not, make sure that the video makes a lasting impression and serves to accomplish brand lift.

An example that's easy to relate to even if you don't use YouTube would be Super Bowl commercials. No advertiser expects to persuade you to get up and go to the store in the middle of the year's biggest football game. What they hope is to make an impression that lasts long enough for you to make that purchase at the next opportunity.

Walmart ran a brilliant ad (which you can easily find online) showing famous sci-fi characters using its grocery pickup, which has resulted in numerous publications making reference to the bit. This has resulted in far more additional views and immeasurable brand lift.

Other Networks

There are many smaller social networks you can advertise on, including some that are extremely popular in different countries or for specific demographic groups.

TikTok, Snapchat, and Twitch, for instance, all support ads. You can even use Facebook Ads Manager to target the Messenger platform, and as of 2020, WhatsApp.

The point is that if your target audience prefers a specific platform, and we haven't already discussed it here, do a little digging and see if they offer advertising solutions. They won't make it hard to find—typically a Google search for "[network name] ads" will result in a direct link to their advertising page. If they don't now, they soon will.

Social networks by their very nature are free to users and therefore must implement a monetization strategy of some kind if they want to survive. Advertising is the model that has been proved to work.

WRAPPING UP

The appeal of paid social media advertising is twofold: It's affordable and measurable.

Regardless of which platform you choose to invest in, it's far more affordable than traditional advertising, and you can track exactly what you received from each dollar you spend—right down to your bottom-line business results.

That means with paid social advertising you have something of a marketing unicorn: true determination of ROI!

If you spend $100 on a Facebook campaign and set up proper tracking for the ad and on your website, you'll see exactly how many visitors it generated and how many purchases resulted. That's pretty cool!

With paid social ads, you can grow your following, reach new audiences, and of course drive traffic and conversions. The purpose of this chapter was to give you a solid understanding of what each platform is capable of. Once you determine the best channel for your business, there are additional resources online you can turn to for more information.

Chapter 10

Leverage Influencer Marketing

In 1903, decades before computers were commercially available, the preferred method of personal communication was the fountain pen. The predecessor to today's ballpoint pens, the fountain pen was elegant, beautiful, and prone to extreme messiness. Those who partook in extended use of such instruments were clearly—and literally—marked.

It was in that year that the Conklin Pen Co. in Toledo, Ohio, decided to employ influencer marketing—though of course it wasn't called that back then. *Influencer marketing* is a relatively recent term. Throughout the 20th century, businesses and marketing agencies turned to celebrities for endorsements and to serve as spokespeople for brands.

In the very early 1900s, most celebrity "influencers" were athletes, and by midcentury movie stars had come on the scene. But Conklin knew not just any old celebrity would do. In order to sell fountain pens to everyday folks, they needed someone everyday folks could relate to, and someone whom it would make sense to tie to the brand.

Imagine if Conklin had hired baseball slugger Babe Ruth as their spokesperson. Other than for signing fat contracts, Babe wasn't known for his use of the quiet quill. While his fans might have taken an interest in Conklin's offerings, few others would have paid it any mind.

So throughout the rest of this chapter, we're going to explore what influencer marketing really means, and how you can identify and work with influencers in your company's niche.

WHAT INFLUENCER MARKETING REALLY MEANS

Put simply, influencer marketing is when a brand leverages someone with an audience of their own to exert some influence over that audience. That might be a recommendation to purchase a product, or it might just entail using the influencer to introduce a brand or business to their audience.

It's important to recognize that *anyone* with an audience is an influencer. Influence is not limited to celebrities with millions of followers on social media. A well-respected member of your community is also an influencer—and, it might be argued, a more powerful one—for the right brand.

We therefore classify potential influencers into a number of categories, depending largely on the size of their audience.

Mega-Influencer

Influencers at this level typically have more than 1 million followers and are usually celebrities outside of social media. Just like the endorsers of the early 1900s, you can expect to see professional athletes and movie stars in this category.

Influencers on this level can generate broad brand awareness and interest over a wide swath of demographics—but you'll pay dearly for that exposure.

Macro-Influencer

Down a tier, we find influencers with between 100,000 and 1 million followers. You'll certainly find your share of real-life celebrities at this level, but you'll also see a great many influencers who have built their influence on social media itself. This includes bloggers, vloggers, and other internet personalities.

It's at this level that we expect to see a far greater degree of specialization or focused interest, such as travel or food, making it a bit easier to find influencers who align with a particular brand.

Micro-Influencer

Even more focused is the micro-influencer, with their 1,000 to 100,000 followers. Of course, someone with nearly 100,000 social media fans could still be said to have a great deal of influence, particularly if they've stayed focused on a specific niche.

It's at this level that brands who are not focused on a specific geographic area (e.g., the Gold Coast of Chicago) can find highly effective and extremely affordable influencers to work with. The challenge when you start to get to influencers in these smaller categories is identifying and working with them. Everyone knows who the mega-celebrities are, and they have experienced staff to handle campaign requests. Joe the Vlogger may have never worked with a brand before, so be prepared for that.

Nano-Influencer

Finally, we have the smallest tier at under 1,000 followers. This is typically where you'll find local influencers who are prominent members of their community. They may even be folks who have limited knowledge and use of social media.

Yet for the right business, a local influencer may be the absolute best choice to work with and drive results. Even a small social following might be ripe with targeted customers in a local setting. And such influencers could be easily incorporated into your own campaigns as a local, recognizable figure.

As you work through the rest of this chapter, begin to think about which categories of influencers might best fit your brand message *and* budget!

HOW TO IDENTIFY INFLUENCERS TO WORK WITH

Just as a Major League Baseball player probably makes for a lousy fountain pen spokesman, so too will most influencers be a poor match for you and your brand.

You need to consider brand fit first before proceeding with any individual influencer.

So what does that mean exactly?

Brand fit is the degree to which a particular influencer's voice, style, audience, and content focus align with that of the representing brand's. In other words, how do the brand and influencer mesh?

It helps if you've already thought about your own brand in terms of style, voice, message, and so on. Taking the time to craft a highly polished style guide (which we discussed in Chapter 6) that considers both aesthetics (fonts, colors, logo treatment) and tone (style, voice, culture, message) will make determining brand fit easier.

The second thing you need to consider is the category of influencer you want to work with (e.g., mega-influencer vs. micro-influencer) and your available budget.

With that in mind, it's time to start looking for influencers. There are a few different approaches you can take. One option is to start with people who are already talking about your brand. These may be customers, bloggers, or other influencers in your industry.

The benefits here are many:

- They are already fans of your brand.
- They may have existing content to amplify.
- They have a track record to evaluate.

And while it's likely these existing fans have smaller audiences and fall in the micro- or nano-influencer category, that means they're probably more affordable.

Another option is to consider the biggest "names" in your industry. These will likely be macro-influencers with established audiences—people who regularly speak at industry events and create content in and about your industry. One reason for starting with known macro-influencers is that it won't take a lot of time to come up with this list. You're probably already following them on social networks like Twitter!

But of course that suggests a third approach, and you'll likely need to do this at some point regardless: research.

Researching possible influencers can take some time but can also be extremely rewarding. It's quite likely you will find some highly influential people who are a great fit for your brand but whom you have never heard of before.

So where do you start?

BuzzSumo, an influencer and content discovery website, is one great option, though you can certainly search Google or individual social platforms directly. When you use BuzzSumo, you can search for influencers specifically on Twitter or Facebook, as well as "authors" who have published content online.

You can filter your results by date, country, or language, and see who some of the most prolific authors for your topic are in ranked order.

Next, drill down to see exactly what they've published and where, and see whether it's really the kind of content where it might make sense to incorporate your brand or products.

If it's a good match, you've found a potential influencer! We'll get into the specifics of what you can do with them later on, but let's first finish considering how to find more potential all-stars.

As you identify possible influencers, we recommend jotting them down in a Google Sheet or a customer resource management tool like Nimble, which will give you easy access to your growing list of contacts and help you learn more about that influencer. With a few clicks, Nimble can scour the web to find their social profiles, websites, contact information, and more. BuzzSumo gives you their Twitter profile, which you can import into Nimble using the Nimble Chrome extension. Tag them as an influencer and return to your research.

If your industry's potential influencers are more likely to be found on YouTube or Instagram, you can search those native platforms or use a tool like Keyword Tool, which will help you search, filter, and sort the results to give you really meaningful information on potential influencers.

Once you begin reaching out to specific influencers, you can ask them to qualify and supplement your research. They can confirm their number of followers, as well as website traffic and email subscribers. More important, if they've worked with other brands in the past, they can share metrics and case studies for the projects they've completed.

It's worth repeating at this point, as we said in Chapter 3, that influencer marketing is all about relationships. We're going to use that word again and again. While you can be purely transactional with an influencer—for instance, fill out a form and pay them to send a tweet—that's not really effective.

Truly effective influencer marketing happens when you establish a relationship with the influencer: when they genuinely like and appreciate your brand and are eager to work with you, and you're eager to work with and support them.

But the thing is . . . relationships take time.

We don't want to say there are no shortcuts to building a great relationship, because we're about to share a bunch of them with you, but none of them will matter unless you can build rapport with each influencer as an individual.

We're stressing this now because you may start doing some research on potential influencers, find a couple, and want to rush into the courtship phase, rather than taking your time to look for more. But you're better off not pinning all your hopes on one person. Take the time to build a great list of potential influencers, and then begin to foster relationships with *all* of them! Some will be open to it, and some won't. Some influencers will be excited to know and work with you, while others will take more time.

These are, essentially, blind dates. And the problem with any relationship is that you *do not know in advance* how it's going to go. One of the people you reach out to today will be the most amazing brand ambassador for you tomorrow, but (and trust us on this) you won't know which one at first.

So if you can, make a list of 25 to 50 potential influencers, and then get to work sparking those relationships.

HOW TO SPARK RELATIONSHIPS

Did we mention relationships take time? We did? Cool. But the good news is that if you proceed deliberately, the odds of creating a mutually successful, beneficial, positive relationship in a shorter amount of time increase dramatically.

But first, a few *don'ts*:

- *Don't* stalk people, especially online influencers.

- *Don't* spam and definitely *don't* add them to email lists without their explicit permission.
- *Don't* have set expectations or demands.
- *Don't* rush.

OK! Now that that's out of the way, let's focus on what you *should* do!

Do Connect

Start by following them on *their* preferred social network. Glance through their various social profiles to see where they're most active and engaged. Note that depending on the network, some follows are one-way and some must be mutually accepted, which means one of you has to initiate the connection and the other must approve it. We'll call the first kind "follow" and the second "connect." Here's a quick rundown:

- Facebook Page: Follow
- Facebook profile: Connect
- Instagram profile: Follow
- LinkedIn profile: Connect
- LinkedIn Page/Influencer: Follow
- Pinterest profile/boards: Follow
- Snapchat profile: Connect
- Twitter profile: Follow
- YouTube channel: Follow

We want to make these distinctions clear because initially, if the influencer doesn't know you, they're not going to be inclined to *connect* with you. It's far easier to simply follow them on Twitter or Instagram, if that's an option.

If their preferred or only social network is one that requires a connection, it may be possible to follow their public posts, depending on the network and their account settings. Or you could bookmark their profile and visit it regularly to see what they've posted.

For nano-influencers who may not be active on social media, consider local organizations they may be involved in, such as Lions Club or the chamber of commerce. You may also want to look for a mutual acquaintance who could introduce you.

Do Engage

Once you have identified and connected with or followed key influencers, it's time to start engaging with them.

On most social networks, you can like/react to posts, share them, and comment on them. You'll need to use your best judgment to determine how to engage with each influencer's post, but here are some helpful guidelines:

- For each influencer, engage with no more than one post per day on average.
- Shares are the most meaningful way to engage: You're saying you trust this person and their content enough to share it with your own audience.
- Comments are an opportunity to open a dialogue that can demonstrate similarities in thought between you and the influencer. This is how you develop rapport.
- Likes and similar reactions are nice for staying top of mind, but are not very meaningful.

You may like, comment on, and share a single post from an influencer, but be wary of doing that too often; similarly, don't like every single post they publish. Some might perceive you as a raving fan, while others might just think you're raving.

Instead, we recommend a daily routine in which you spend just 30 to 60 minutes checking in on the activity of your target influencers and engaging when it makes sense to do so, in as natural a way as possible.

This is another area where Nimble can be incredibly powerful. As you identify influencers and begin to import them into Nimble, you can use tags to signify the stage of your relationship with them.

Let's say you have a "New" tag for influencers you're just starting to connect with. Within Nimble's Contacts area, you can search only for contacts labeled "New" and then scroll through that list. For each one, you can see your past engagements and other pertinent information, and you can click through to their social profiles to see if they've posted recently. You might add other labels for "engaged" or even "under contract" that you would change contact tags within Nimble and perhaps engage less or treat differently over time.

While you can create other mechanisms like Twitter Lists to follow multiple people, they can be easily overwhelmed by prolific posters. Using Nimble to jump to each influencer's social profiles will save you time, and you can easily stop in the middle of the process to handle another business task and then pick it up again later.

Do Observe

As you are building rapport with each influencer, you should also be observing how they meet your third requirement: *audience engagement*.

It is quite possible for someone to have a large social media following and yet exert very little influence. Their followers might have been purchased, or the influencer may have had an engaged audience at one time but now, due to a variety of reasons, their followers have lost interest.

As you're engaging with an influencer's posts and content, take note of how much more engagement they get. Are you the only one commenting? Are the same people commenting every time? Or are a nice variety of people engaging with the influencer and a decent number of people being reached?

And, in turn, how does the influencer respond to comments? Do they ignore you and everyone else? Or do they take the time to respond to every comment and keep their audience engaged? What is the tone of those responses? If they were replying to a comment while representing your brand, how comfortable would you be?

If you're observant, you will pick up on their perspectives when it comes to business, your industry, and other aspects of life that are important to you and *your* audience. You'll come to understand their worldview, and that will help you relate to them.

Make observations, take notes, and use your intuition as to whether a particular influencer is a good fit for your brand and marketing program—you'll usually be spot on. You can also go the more formal route of creating a spreadsheet and scoring system for each influencer you observe. If you're reporting to a CMO or department head, this would be a good way to document and establish the value of your effort.

After you have spent a while engaging with key influencers and they've responded positively, it's time for you to reach out and propose a new stage of your relationship: collaboration.

HOW TO WORK WITH INFLUENCERS

Mike is the Brand Evangelist at Agorapulse, where his approach with social media influencers is to gift them a free lifetime account with the company's social media management software and see if they like using it. He can see whether they're logging into the app or talking about Agorapulse online; if they are, he deepens the relationship by amplifying their content, sending them swag, and inviting them to participate in marketing activities like roundups or webinars, where everyone benefits.

Thinkific, which makes online learning software, has a very similar, extremely successful approach. Their Community Manager gives prominent influencers free access to Thinkific's course platform and ships them Thinkific hoodies to sport on social media (which gets the company even more attention!).

When Mike or Thinkific want to do a live show and need a guest, or want to run a virtual summit of webinars, they have a large pool of talented experts and influencers on hand to tap.

Unpaid Collaboration

If possible and appropriate for your business, this strategy of giving away free products or services is an excellent first step toward working with influencers, as there is mutual benefit and typically little to no cost to the brand.

For example, suppose you want to create a piece of content around a topic that is relevant to your brand and/or industry, perhaps one that answers a question many of your target prospects are struggling with. While you could write the entire post from your own perspective, it might instead be better to reach out to 20 or 30 influencers in your space and invite them to answer the question, publishing the results as a roundup. Here are three benefits of this strategy:

1. Roundup posts share varying perspectives and opinions.
2. Roundup posts with 20-plus participants will be epic in length due to the sheer number of participants. Even if the average response is just 150 words long, that will be more than 3,000 words for the overall post.
3. Roundup posts with 20-plus participants will be shared far more than usual, as most participating influencers will naturally share the post with their own networks, thereby significantly increasing the post's visibility.

When you publish a roundup post, your job is to make your influencers look amazing. Take the time to create nice graphics and "influencer cards" featuring their name, head shot, and Twitter handle. Once it's published, make sure they're all tagged on your social posts so they'll help you amplify the content and get your blog in front of their audiences.

It's a win-win.

Paid Collaboration

The next level of influencer collaboration is some sort of paid campaign. What that campaign looks like, and of course what the compensation is, will vary a great deal.

While you might be tempted to fork out large amounts of cash to get a mega-influencer to mention you in a tweet, a better option would be to build longer-lasting campaigns with influencers with smaller, but more targeted, audiences.

For example:

- Shoot a testimonial video.
- Write a blog post.
- Participate in a Facebook Live interview.
- Publish a review.
- Talk about your brand in their newsletter.

Generally, we recommend making a note of what each influencer tends to do and then coming up with an idea for a campaign format that fits their natural approach.

If, for instance, they excel at Instagram, perhaps create a series of image-centered posts or Stories that will educate their audience on your brand in a fun and interesting way—and one that matches their usual style.

The trick is to come up with a campaign that has as many of the following advantages as possible:

- It runs long enough to ensure brand exposure to a wide audience.
- It's short enough to limit investment and initial risk.
- It educates audiences about your brand/product(s).
- It entertains audiences and keeps them engaged.
- It results in assets that can be repurposed or reused.

Let's say you want a micro-influencer to talk about your brand on social media and introduce you to their network. Rather than a single tweet or post, you might come up with a specific topic that is important to that influencer and relevant to your brand, and devise a series of posts and activities centered on that topic.

That might include shares of relevant and engaging articles—yours or other people's, mentions of your brand and products, determining key hashtags, and perhaps a live video to finish the campaign.

At the end of that campaign, you'll have reached a sizable portion of the influencer's audience, driven traffic to your web properties, gained new social media followers, and created a piece of video content you can repurpose to use elsewhere in any number of ways.

Compensation

When it comes to compensation for influencers, brands have a lot of options and room to be creative. While a mega-influencer requires a contract and a significant cash payout, everyone else will be a lot more affordable.

That starts at free.

Many smaller influencers will be happy to work with you in exchange for free products, services, or access; co-marketing; and collaboration. In fact, many retail brands collaborate with micro- and nano-influencers simply by offering a discount on products.

The trick is to balance generosity with practicality. Come up with a variety of ways to work with and help influencers and then weigh what you're prepared to offer against what you expect to receive in return. Options include:

- Free products/services/access

- Upgraded services or access
- Corporate swag and gifts
- Behind-the-scenes/direct access to point people
- Affiliate commissions
- Increased affiliate commissions
- One-time payments
- Ongoing payments

Make sure that however you approach your influencer marketing and specific influencers, you set aside time to review the program and your measurables either monthly or quarterly. Don't just assume it's working. It's helpful to have that discussion with individual influencers as well. Is there anything else you can do for them that might make them even more vocal in support of your brand?

INFLUENCER MARKETING ADMINISTRATIVE DETAILS

While creating campaigns can be a lot of fun, the way you run your initiatives and influencer marketing program must be organized and thorough.

Use Contracts

You might not want or think you need to use contracts with your influencers, but you must have your relationship in writing once money starts to change hands. If you communicate upfront how the business aspects of the relationship will work, you can avoid potential friction that might jeopardize the entire connection.

That said, you don't need complex contracts filled with legal language, particularly when dealing with micro- and nano-influencers. In most cases, it is sufficient to document how you will compensate the influencer and what your brand will receive in exchange.

The more experience an influencer has working with brands, the more comfortable they will be with formal contracts. It's best to raise the issue early on and talk briefly about setting out the requirements for both parties.

Set Expectations

For each campaign, clearly document all agreed-upon expectations. These will typically include activity, time frame, frequency, assets needed or to be created, and any given performance metrics.

For example: "X social posts over X weeks to Facebook, Instagram, and Twitter, using images and copy provided by the influencer."

Manage Projects

Once everyone agrees on the nature and scope of the campaign, it's time to move on to project management. It's usually best to use a project management tool like Asana, because you can create campaign templates for yourself and duplicate them for each project and influencer as needed. However, something as simple as a Google Doc can work, too.

The key is to make sure everything is considered and communicated in advance. If other people have tasks they need to do, make sure they understand what's required and by when so that everything can be delivered on time.

Pay Promptly

When it comes to dealing with online influencers, prompt and full payment is essential. The last thing you want is an upset influencer with 100,000 followers ruining your reputation with a series of negative tweets.

Of course, you want to get what you paid for, and if an influencer agreed to a contract and didn't deliver, they shouldn't get paid. But never withhold payment if the results weren't quite what you hoped for, or perhaps a deliverable didn't arrive on time. You should be generous and magnanimous at this stage, and recognize the truth of influencer marketing: Working to improve brand awareness simply cannot be measured. Any activity on the part of influencers will be valuable and long-lasting.

That leads us into the final topic we need to consider when it comes to influencer marketing: success.

WHAT INFLUENCER MARKETING SUCCESS LOOKS LIKE

At the beginning of the chapter, we talked about how the Conklin Pen Co. wanted to connect with a contemporary influencer to endorse their fountain pens. Who do you think they might have gone with in 1903, someone who fits all the criteria we've talked about?

They decided on famous author Mark Twain.

Twain was the writer of "*The Adventures of Huckleberry Finn, The Adventures of Tom Sawyer, Life on the Mississippi*, and *A Connecticut Yankee in King Arthur's Court*. He was extremely well-known throughout the country as someone who *penned* his thoughts regularly. Clearly, Twain could easily be seen using and enjoying a fountain pen.

And so he was paid to endorse the Conklin Crescent pen and was quoted as saying, "I prefer it to ten other fountain pens because it carries its filler in its own stomach, and I cannot mislay it even by art or intention. Also, I prefer it because it is a profanity saver; it cannot roll off the desk."

His quotes and endorsements not only contributed to greater awareness of Conklin pens and doubtless more sales, but also represented assets the company was able to repurpose for half a century.

That engagement of an influencer was clearly a success for Conklin, whatever the cost. But how can you determine if your influencer marketing is successful?

Tip of the Iceberg

Because of the density of icebergs, they float through the ocean with just a small portion visible above the water. All you can see is a small tip, even though the entire iceberg may be huge.

THINK INSIDE THE BOX

Most people think influencer marketing is all about spending a lot of money with celebrities chasing vanity metrics. This couldn't be further from the truth. As I clearly outline in my book *The Age of Influence*, the democratization of media influence means that there are simply a lot more people who wield influence over other people, due to the mainstream maturation of social media, than ever before. This means that influence is all around us, so instead of thinking outside the box when considering influencers to collaborate with, think inside the box: employees, partners, fans and followers, customers, etc. There are probably a lot of people who already have a tremendous amount of brand affinity for your company who would love to collaborate with you.

Another myth about influencer marketing is that it is just for big consumer brands. But any business, no matter how small and regardless of industry, can find, engage with, and collaborate with other social media users and generate a win-win relationship. It comes down to developing relationships with social media users who influence potential customers and working together in a way that benefits both of you. It also means treating each influencer as an individual. Every influencer is different when it comes to what they would like from a brand collaboration, so stay open-minded while being very specific about what you would like the influencer to do on your behalf. You will never know the best incentive to get them to work with you if you don't ask!

—Neal Schaffer, author of *The Age of Influence: The Power of Influencers to Elevate Your Brand* (HarperCollins Leadership, 2020)

Measuring influencer marketing is the same. There are some things you can measure, such as *reach* (how many people saw a particular post), *clicks* (traffic sent from a post to linked assets), *leads*, and *sales*. Any campaign can make use of UTM parameters to fully attribute results, which we'll go into detail on within Chapter 13.

What you can't measure is the number of people who were introduced to your brand or products by an influencer and decide to purchase days or even weeks later. You also can't measure how people's perceptions change (hopefully for the better) due to that influencer's efforts.

Simply put, this is *brand awareness*. The more people know and talk about your brand, the more likely they will be to think of or consider your brand when the need arises.

It's impossible to measure accurately, but when it's executed well, your business should see improvements to the most important metric of all—your bottom line.

Chapter 11

Repurpose and Reuse Social Content

In this chapter, we're going to talk about how to turn social media activity into valuable website content, or content for other channels.

Specifically, we'll cover five different techniques that you can pick and choose from, or even use them all! Coupled with articles you write to help educate your audience, these techniques can fuel your blog and drive your content marketing efforts indefinitely.

But before we get into all that, we'd like to tell you a story about a movie.

In 1999, Touchstone Pictures released *The 13th Warrior*, an adaptation of a Michael Crichton novel (*Eaters of the Dead*) about an exiled Arab poet traveling into northern Europe and his adventure alongside a group of Viking warriors. The movie is filled with action, suspense, and interesting dialogue from Antonio Banderas as the poet, Ahmad ibn Fadlan.

We've always enjoyed the film, and particularly liked the great Omar Sharif's minor role as Ahmad's guide. But it was a complete disaster.

Production of the film cost $160 million, but it brought in only $61.7 million at the box office. That movie lost Touchstone $100 million! Yikes! Its reception was so bad that Sharif largely retired from acting for several years, saying, "Bad pictures are very humiliating."

We share that story because it's an important contrast for what we're going to be talking about today. Filmmaking is a risky business. Studios gamble millions of dollars on each production.

Blog posts, while low-cost, can still seem high-risk to us. You can spend hours, sometimes days, slaving over an article, only to publish it and watch it sink without a ripple of response.

Was it that poorly written? Or was it simply on a subject your audience had no interest in?

In this chapter, we're not just going to talk about how you can save time by turning social media content into website content; we'll also show you how careful selection of content mitigates risk.

Let's say you have a Facebook post that went viral and a tweet that got no engagement whatsoever. Which do you think will perform better as part of a blog post?

The viral one, of course!

While there are many reasons one social post might outperform another, the one reason we can reliably count on when creating subsequent pieces of content is the topic.

As we go through the following five techniques, please bear that in mind. When you have a choice, always select from the most successful social posts and use the native engagement indicators, such as likes and shares, to guide you.

Ready to take some notes? Let's begin.

TECHNIQUE 1: LIVE VIDEO

This is perhaps our favorite technique, and one we've used countless times. Whether you wish to use Facebook Live, YouTube, Periscope, Instagram, or some other platform, live video is an opportunity for you to broadcast yourself, and perhaps one or more other people, and be seen by a live audience. (You first read about the joys of live video in Chapter 7.)

If it were simply recorded video of you sharing your thoughts, it would be little different from a blog post—just in a different medium. Live video, however, has additional aspects and benefits.

For one thing, since you can broadcast with other people on most social media platforms, you can bring guests and experts into your video who will help you create the content. Instead of relying solely on your own expertise, you can capitalize on the depth of knowledge these guests possess, whether it's a live discussion, interview, or Q&A.

Additionally, the fact that you have a live audience can actually help you create content. Throughout the broadcast, you can read comments left by viewers and bring those comments into the broadcast as questions to be answered.

In fact, some brands and broadcasters devote an entire broadcast to answering audience questions; the video is entirely unscripted and requires very little preparation as a result.

Once your video is over, that's when the real magic happens. Let's assume that you have decided to broadcast to Facebook using an app like Ecamm or StreamYard so you can bring in guests easily (as we discussed in Chapter 7). You've spent 30 minutes interviewing an expert in your industry, and now the broadcast is done.

You now have a 30-minute video that you can download as an MP4 file. At an average speaking rate of 150 words per minute, that video can be transcribed into roughly a 4,500-word blog post! If the average blog post is 750 words, and blog posts that are 2,000-plus words perform best, how well do you think a 4,500-word blog post is going to do?

However, if you're sticking to your original principle of only using successful social posts, that means that before you transcribe and publish this video as a blog post, make sure it was a good video. Were there more viewers than usual? Were there great comments and discussion? Did you and your guests engage in a lively debate? Whatever your barometer for success is, make sure it applies before you take this extra step.

Once you have the transcript (and inexpensive transcription services like Rev.com and Quicc.io are available to help with that), you can publish it as a blog post with just a brief introduction explaining what people are about to read. You can also embed the original video along with it, which serves two purposes:

1. Visitors to the blog may prefer to watch the video rather than read the post, which adds 30 minutes to their time on the site.
2. Anyone who engages with the video by liking or commenting on it will create a story in their feed for their friends to see.

There are even more possibilities. You can strip the audio track from the video and turn that into a separate podcast. If you pull short segments of the audio into an app like Headliner, you can create audiograms—basically video files that use a static image with an audio track. You can slice out specific segments of the video and use them for social posts or as the basis for additional blog posts.

Suppose, for instance, that you and your expert talked about a specific topic for five minutes and answered a couple of viewer questions. That segment alone is probably valuable enough to upload separately to Facebook or YouTube. And depending on the topic, it might be worth expanding on it in an article of its own.

Finally, take note of any specific comments your guests make that are truly brilliant and turn those into quotes or even quote graphics that, again, you can use within blog posts or other social media stories.

TECHNIQUE 2: USER-GENERATED CONTENT

While the first technique relied on video content that you created yourself, this technique gets to use posts that you had nothing to do with.

Posts that other people create, which we then use for our own business, are called user-generated content. While it's most often used in reference to content other people create about our business, such as video testimonials, it doesn't have to be limited to that.

One popular example these days is news articles about a trending topic that consist mostly of tweets from other people about that topic: "So-and-so did something stupid and the internet has gone crazy about it." The story has one or two paragraphs about the actual event and then half a dozen tweets from random people sharing their opinions.

That technique might work very well if you work in an industry in which there are often big news events on which people are commenting publicly. Send a quick direct message asking for permission to use their tweet in a story, grab the embed code Twitter provides, and you have a nice blog post.

But what if nothing much newsworthy happens in your industry?

There's nothing wrong with using posts that really are about your business in some way, even if they aren't news, so watch for those. Also watch for great comments on your other blog posts or social posts.

You could also look for blog posts and articles written by others and reference or curate those. For instance, suppose someone writes a blog about the "10 Best Providers of X" and names your business in that list. You could summarize and link to that article in a blog post of your own.

The point is to always be on the lookout for content that other people create on their own sites, in your blog comments, or on social networks that's either directly about your business or about your industry in general, and think about how you might use it. Using content generated by other users and customers is a great way to make connections with them and the rest of your target audience!

TECHNIQUE 3: EMBEDDED SOCIAL MEDIA POSTS

In the first technique, we mentioned you can embed the recorded video from Facebook or YouTube into a blog post with the video's transcript. In the second technique, we talked about how to embed tweets or other social posts from other people into a blog to help create a story. How else might we use and embed social posts?

First, social media posts make great examples, even if you're not talking about the post itself. We'll explain.

Let's say you're a business that provides a service to people that you can take pictures of, whether it's cutting hair, building decks, or something else.

Now, you could write a blog post about a particular project and just embed the pictures into that article. But why not leverage the power of social media instead? Post the pictures to your Facebook Page before you publish your article and then embed the Facebook post into your blog post.

Just like with embedded videos, any kind of embedded social post will benefit from the additional views and engagement it receives from your blog readers.

In fact, there's nothing stopping you from using this technique on older content as well. Let's say you have an article from a couple of years ago that still gets good search engine traffic. Take a few moments to update that article and embed a relevant Facebook video or photo album, and watch as those social posts get renewed interest from your organic traffic.

Another way to use this technique is to use social media to poll or survey your audience and then embed that post into an article that talks about the topic and shares the results of the poll. We'll come back to this idea in Technique 5.

TECHNIQUE 4: TURN DISCUSSIONS INTO BLOG POSTS

While turning live video into blog content might be our favorite technique, turning discussions into blog posts might be the one we've had the most long-term success with.

How often have you commented on a Facebook or Instagram post, or participated in a discussion on Twitter? All the time, right? Real, back-and-forth conversations is what social networks are designed for.

Now, if you're like us, a lot of those discussions have been professional, as many of our social connections are peers and colleagues. We'll talk about what's happening with Instagram shadow bans, or what's going to happen to third-party video tools when Facebook finishes integrating all the needed functions with Creator Studio. We also talk to other business owners and readers who want to know about something in our niche and answer their questions.

While doing all this, we have trained ourselves to automatically think about a potential blog post whenever we find ourselves spending more than a couple of minutes on an answer. If one person on Facebook wants to know about something relating to your business or industry, there are likely many other people who want to know that same information.

In those instances, we've found the best option is to post our comment and conclude the discussion, and then copy and paste all the relevant text into an Evernote note. That way we can easily find it later and decide whether it would really make for a good blog post.

TECHNIQUE 5: ASK QUESTIONS

Finally, the one technique that we see far too few bloggers and marketers use is to *ask questions!* Just *ask* your audience what they want to know about!

As long as you've been making even the slightest effort to have real conversations with your growing audience, some of your followers will have questions.

Sometimes they'll be quick questions you can answer in a brief comment. Sometimes they'll be questions you've already answered, which is a perfect opportunity to share a link to an article and impress them with your expertise.

Sometimes they'll be questions you haven't answered that require a little space to address. Those are perfect subjects for videos or blog posts! And not only are those questions the source of blog content, but you can also embed the original social post within the blog, as we described in Technique 3 above.

The beauty of this technique is twofold. First, you don't have to worry about not getting enough questions. Most of us only have enough time to create new articles two to four times a month, so one or two great questions once in a while is fabulous!

Second, since someone else asked the question, you know there's at least one person interested in the answer! Too often our ideas for blog posts are spun out of the void between our ears, which means we're gambling with our time, just like Touchstone Pictures did with *The 13th Warrior*.

Your time is one of your most valuable commodities. You don't want to squander it creating content that no one cares about. When you begin to leverage all the types of social media content available to you, you can mitigate that risk and even create terrific synergies between your blog and social media.

Chapter 12

Build Your Marketing Team

Michael Jordan, six-time NBA champion and NBA Finals MVP, once said, "Talent wins games, but teamwork and intelligence win championships." Jordan obviously knows a thing or two about playing sports, but what about business? Does that quote really apply to a book about social media?

Yes. Yes it does.

You see, up until this point, you've probably been handling things yourself, and that hasn't been too bad. Whatever your strengths and deficiencies, you're informed and equipped to accommodate those traits.

But your time, experience, and resources aren't infinite. If you want to continue to grow your business, you must find ways to scale up your marketing efforts. Throughout the rest of this chapter, we're going to throw a *ton* of information at you—not in an attempt to educate you on everything you need to know about employing others (there are entire books about that), but rather to give you specific points to consider when building your social media marketing team, whether you want to build that team now or sometime in the future. This will help you determine what form your team should take, how it should be composed, and what tools and processes you may need to put into place.

From there, you'll be better-equipped to do additional research or even obtain professional consulting on the areas in which you need more information.

For instance, we'll talk about whether to hire employees or contractors, or outsource to an agency entirely. What we *won't* talk about is things like tax considerations and employment benefits as they pertain to direct hires. That's beyond the scope of this book.

You will come out of this chapter armed with an understanding of how to scale your marketing, and our best advice and recommendations on how to accomplish that.

Let's dive in.

INTERNAL VS. EXTERNAL TEAM

The first consideration when it comes to putting together your social media team—that group of superheroes who will stay on top of your messaging and online conversations day and night—is whether you want it to be internal to your business or an external agency.

An internal team is an opportunity for you to completely control the narrative. Your team comes up with every post, message, and piece of dialogue, and can craft them to meet your needs exactly. If you use an external team, you have to spend more time communicating your brand message and reviewing what the agency comes up with.

An external team is likely composed of individuals with very specific skill sets and experience working on similar projects. This is one way to avoid the very real problem of assigning unfamiliar tasks to inexperienced employees.

If it's an internal team, they report to you and no one else. They do not have other clients competing for their time or creative energy. If you need them to spend more time on a particular campaign or project, they will. An external team will likely have a negotiated budget of time and resources that are allocated to you each month.

By hiring an external team, you gain the benefit of that team's industry experience. They may have worked for many other clients in your vertical or geographic region and be able to tap that knowledge in a way that is beyond the grasp of an internal team.

As you can see, there are benefits and challenges to either approach. From a cost perspective, there are affordable options for both internal and external teams. Internally, you can use part-time help or hire one full-time employee to handle multiple roles. Externally, you can contract an inexpensive solopreneur or small firm at first.

One important note about that expense, however. If you haven't previously hired media professionals for your business, you may be in for an eye-opening experience.

Let's do a quick exercise. How much do you bill per hour when invoicing your time? (If you sell products, consider how much product you can sell in an hour if you're actively promoting it.)

Now take careful note of how much time you spend every day, week, and month on specific tasks. Write them down on a piece of paper divided in half: on one side are the things that directly help you make that hourly rate; on the other side is everything else.

What's on that other side? What are those tasks costing you? Whether it's doing the accounting or cleaning the office or mowing the lawn, you should be able to delegate that task to someone else (who makes less per hour than you do) and free up that time for yourself to make more money.

Your marketing efforts can be viewed the same way. If you can delegate some or all of the business marketing to someone who costs less per hour than you can earn, you'll be ahead! In other words, if marketing isn't in your creative zone of genius, hire someone else to do it!

Now, whether you go with an internal or external team, it will be critical to overcommunicate with them. Your marketing plans and initiatives will now happen outside your head, and your staff cannot know what you're thinking unless you make it clear to them.

Go back through the earlier chapters of this book and use them to craft a plan and strategy. Document it and discuss it with your team. We'll also be sharing some tools, processes, and best practices to help you with that in a moment.

As long as you have your strategy in place, that's your north star. It's what you and your team are always working toward.

TEAM ROLES

Every good team needs to have roles. The basketball teams Michael Jordan played on were always structured the same. There was a point guard, a shooting guard, a small forward, a power forward, and a center. Successful startups often follow the model of a visionary, an engineer, and a salesperson.

Similarly, your social media marketing team needs to perform a number of critical jobs. It is possible for one person to assume some or even all these roles, though, as we'll demonstrate in a moment. That will largely depend on expertise and availability.

Strategist

The social media strategist is similar to the entrepreneur or visionary role in certain business models. They determine the direction and message for all social media efforts, and are typically in charge of the team.

They will decide which platforms to focus on, what tactics to employ, and what the overall goals and expectations for the team and initiatives will be.

Community Manager

The community manager is responsible for monitoring and engaging with all incoming communication from your brand's audience, regardless of network, platform, or medium. This includes comments on posts, direct messages, live videos, and conversations with chatbots.

They will likely be responsible for all outgoing posts and activity as well, though that responsibility may be shared with the strategist.

Analyst

The analyst is responsible for reviewing and reporting on all available metrics, as well as determining what can be measured and what steps should be taken to ensure solid metrics are available.

They may, for instance, provide the community manager with specific tracking links to use in certain campaigns so that the back-end reporting can successfully attribute all mediums and initiatives.

Advertising Manager

The advertising manager is responsible for all paid advertising—typically Facebook and Google ads, as we discussed in Chapter 9.

In conjunction with the strategist, they will create ad campaigns designed to deliver very specific results. They'll design the assets, audiences, and campaigns and then monitor their performance on a daily basis. They may also work with the community manager to potentially boost organic social posts that are already performing well.

Social Media Manager

The social media manager is all these roles combined into one. They have the experience, skills, and time to create strategy, implement tactics, monitor channels, handle paid advertising, and monitor results.

For many small to midsize businesses, this is how you begin to build a team. You hire a social media manager first and gradually separate their roles as you add team members. Again, you may never want or need to hire individuals for each specific role.

Depending on the needs of your business, existing employees may assume some of these roles alongside their other responsibilities. An email and outbound marketing specialist might also handle your paid advertising. A data analyst who is running your business analytics may also help with social media marketing metrics.

As long as someone has been assigned these roles and understands how they fit into your overall marketing and brand-building teams, you will have the team you need.

ASSEMBLING YOUR TEAM

As we said at the outset, topics like employee handbooks and health benefits are more than we can cover in a book about social media marketing. However, there are some basic differences between hiring contractors and full-time employees, or bringing on an agency or virtual assistants, that we should mention here.

If you're prepared to hire someone internally to fill one or more of the above roles, you will need to publish a job description and opening, interview prospects, and ultimately select a candidate. You must research comparable pay in your region to determine what a fair offer for that role would be.

A contractor is someone who charges you a set fee for their work and has a contract that states deliverables, timing, requirements, and fees. A contractor has their own business, whether an LLC or sole proprietorship, and is paid via invoice.

Using a contractor for some of your social media marketing may be an attractive solution, particularly if you can find someone with the right fit, as hiring someone typically carries higher costs and additional administrative requirements.

Every state has its own laws and regulations with regard to contract work. Check with applicable websites, organizations, and your accountant to make sure you accomplish all required steps.

Is your business seasonal? Are your requirements less than part time? If so, hiring a contractor may be an excellent solution.

Another option is using a virtual assistant (VA) for some of your marketing efforts. Depending on the VA, they may be able to help with content curation, transcription, scheduling and publishing, and other repetitive tasks.

VAs are most commonly found outside the United States, which leads to lower costs, fewer regulations, and the benefit of being able to cover a much wider range of time zones.

If there are community colleges or universities near you, inquire about potential interns. A marketing student could be a perfect assistant for your social media manager or strategist, if they need help covering some other tasks and can take the time to train interns to do the work.

Whether you're hiring internally or contracting externally, be prepared to create a formal contract along with a nondisclosure agreement (NDA), which stipulates that they may not discuss any of your plans or information. And you should definitely include within the contract stipulations regarding what is and is not intellectual property.

For instance, if your community manager writes an ebook for your lead generation tactic, he is free to republish that work after he has left the company.

Consult your attorney when crafting these documents to ensure full protection and clarity for all involved.

If, however, you plan to employ an agency or other outside vendors for any aspect of your marketing, someone on your team needs to take on the role of account manager.

The account manager is responsible for determining a vendor's deliverables, cost, and time frame; for communicating all requirements to that vendor; and for regularly checking in with that vendor to receive updates on progress. Without a dedicated account manager monitoring the vendor relationship, weeks or even months could go by before you realize there's an issue that needs to be addressed.

But before you hire anyone, you need to amp up your own documentation.

TEAM DOCUMENTATION AND SUPPORT

It's quite possible that "documentation" is Stephanie's favorite word, rivaled only by "dim sum."

With complete documentation, you create a mechanism to teach and onboard new team members, communicate plans and expectations, and give everyone the ability to read and comprehend those important instructions at their own pace.

This documentation is critical, but it doesn't have to be complicated. A set of shared Google Docs will work just fine. And it's OK to create initial documentation that then changes and evolves over time.

This documentation can include, but is not limited to:

- *Style guide.* The style guide, or brand kit as some call it, collects all design requirements, restrictions, and elements into one place for easy reference. This should include your logo and all specified treatments (e.g., color vs. white, square vs. rectangle), your fonts, and your specific brand colors. As we discussed in Chapter 6, your team can use Photoshop, Canva, or Easil to create graphics, and these specifications can often be included within the apps or templates.
- *Branding guide.* A better name for this might be *messaging*, as this includes elements of your brand and business that aren't in the style guide, such as mission, vision, and voice. *How* you talk to your audience is often as important as what you say. (Refer back to Chapter 6 for a refresher on this.)
- *Day-to-day schedule.* This helps outline your daily tasks, particularly for the community manager and advertising manager, who will have daily responsibilities that cannot be neglected.

- *Expectations.* Often incorporated into a document unique to each hire and role, this makes crystal clear what you expect of each employee. You should give them the courtesy of being able to discuss and help shape those expectations.
- *Expenses and reimbursement.* Make it clear from the outset what expenses are expected and what will be reimbursed. Will you cover your community manager's data plan so they can continue monitoring your social media activity from their mobile phone? Will you cover travel and meals to requested events? Decide these issues as well as a method for reporting and reimbursement so there are no surprises or bruised feelings (and wallets).
- *Onboarding guide.* Whether you're hiring internally or outsourcing, you need to have a documented process of onboarding so that no necessary step is overlooked. And as you walk through this process with a new team member, make a note of any changes, corrections, or omissions since the last time so that each iteration can be improved.

This should include access to tools and networks. In fact, consider using a password tool like LastPass, which can facilitate sharing access information. As part of this process, make a note of how each tool or network allows shared access. Facebook, for instance, has you give an existing Facebook user administrative access to your page, whereas Twitter has no such capability and requires you to simply share usernames and passwords.

The onboarding guide should also be used or duplicated as an offboarding guide. Whether an employee is leaving or an agency's contract isn't being renewed, make sure you revoke their access and complete other tasks accordingly. Having a checklist for everything you need to do ensures business efficiency and transferability of operations.

RECOMMENDED TOOLS

Fortunately, there are lots of available tools to help you and your team accomplish all this—and more. We already mentioned Google Docs for documentation and Agorapulse for social media management, which includes built-in team functionality. Below are a few more tools you can use to meet your team's needs:

- *Hiring.* Workable is a great way to manage your entire hiring process. From posting resumes to interviewing candidates, it gives you full control and visibility over the process.
- *Project management.* Project management is an essential part of the process, particularly when collaborating with remote or external teams, and Asana is typically what we use and recommend. Basecamp and Trello are also excellent options.

- *Communication.* Every member of the team will of course have email and a phone, but with Slack, you can group clients or conversations into different channels, send notifications or files as needed, and even integrate video calling, which is of paramount importance for distributed teams.
- *Calendaring.* For the most part, a shared Google Calendar is the preferred medium for tracking meetings and events and coordinating schedules. It can automatically integrate with Google Meet to facilitate team video calls: an inexpensive group video platform that supports up to one hundred participants.
- *Training and information.* You and your team have quite a few choices when it comes to keeping up-to-date with the latest in social media. You can read blogs, attend events, and consume weekly marketing shows and podcasts that keep their audiences updated.
  - Blogs include *Social Media Examiner*, *Social Media Today*, and *Marketing Land*. You can follow *Jenn's Trends*, *The Digital Gal*, *Hey Stephanie*, and *The Social Media Hat*. And you can tune in to shows like Agorapulse's Facebook Live show *Social Pulse Weekly*.
  - Social Media Marketing World in San Diego and the Midwest Digital Marketing Conference in St. Louis are two popular events to attend.

Social media is always changing, as we've said repeatedly throughout this book. Have processes and people in place to help you manage it, but also mechanisms so you can keep learning. You don't need to leap to adopt every shiny new trend or app, but you *should* have an understanding of where social media marketing is headed so you can ensure your efforts are properly aligned.

Keeping an eye on trends and on the future of social media marketing, while regularly checking in with your team and monitoring analytics, will sometimes lead you to the conclusion that you need to make a change.

Maybe things aren't going so well, or maybe you see an opportunity. Whatever the case, what do you do when it's time to pivot?

That's what we're going to address in the final chapter. But first, let's take a closer look at how you can measure what you're doing.

Chapter 13

Measure Success

In line with the goals we determined earlier, you will need to be able to track the success of your marketing efforts. But what does that success look like, and what tools or processes can you put in place to facilitate it?

Let's start by defining some of the key metrics:

- *Traffic*. This is where everyone should start. Simply sign up for a free Google Analytics account and make sure it's connected to your website. Once that's in place, you can use the account to see not only how much traffic is coming to your site, but also where it's coming from, how long it's staying, and what it's doing while it's there.

- *Conversions*. The easiest way to track conversions is to create a thank-you or confirmation page once a visitor has completed the conversion action. You can then set up a goal within Google Analytics to track that page. If you're operating an ecommerce system that Google Analytics recognizes, it will record and report product sales and revenue automatically.

- *Leads*. You have lots of options when it comes to lead management and email marketing. The obvious recommendation is usually to use Mailchimp. You can add a signup form or page to your site with whatever offer you want and track how many people choose to subscribe. And for new businesses with small lists, Mailchimp is free.

■ *Social media.* What you can track and how you can track it will vary depending on which social network(s) you start with. Some, like Facebook, offer built-in analytics with their business accounts. Others, like LinkedIn, really don't tell you much at all, particularly if you're leveraging a personal profile and not a business page. If you need more than the network offers, consider using a third-party tool like Agorapulse.

In this chapter, we're going to give you a baseline understanding of analytics, including the difference between qualitative and quantitative metrics, and then review the available tools that will help you measure the success of your social media efforts.

UNDERSTANDING ANALYTICS

We'll review what the various networks offer and what to look for in a moment, but first, let's talk about how to understand the analytics you are given.

Reading and comprehending the analytics reports that are available to you on social media sites is really more of an art than a science. That's because the reports contain only raw data, and it's up to you to apply context.

For instance, what if we told you that a certain blog post received 200-plus social signals last week and more than 240 visitors, and that out of those visitors, there were a dozen new leads. Is that good or bad? The conversion rate sounds good, but the overall traffic might seem poor. Just 240 visitors? But if you learned that the site itself was just three weeks old and this was the first blog post it had promoted, the traffic seems more reasonable—perhaps even great!

That's context, and while you must apply it to everything you read and see, it's challenging to know what context to apply and when. Often there are variables affecting the data that we're unaware of.

This is incredibly important whenever people start sharing real data with you about their blogs and social channels. They'll talk about thousands of visitors per month or tens of thousands of followers, but what you need to keep firmly in mind is how long they've been running, how much content they've created, the other marketing methods they've employed during that time, and what industry they're in!

With that perspective, watch your daily, weekly, and monthly statistics. Over time, which pages get more traffic than others? Can you improve them? Do you need to do something about your other, less popular pages? Where does most of your traffic come from? Which social posts and channels get the most engagement? What techniques or hashtags have the greatest impact? Look for opportunities to capitalize on what you're getting and build on areas that can be improved.

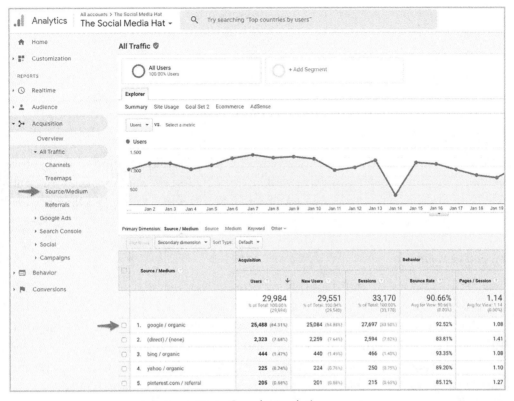

FIGURE 13–1. Google Analytics report

For instance, you should routinely keep an eye on which blog posts are getting good, organic referral traffic from Google. To do this, in Google Analytics, click on the Acquisition report, go to All Traffic, and then go to Source/Medium. Find "google/organic" listed in the table and see what the referral traffic was for the given time frame (see Figure 13–1).

When you see some of your content start to get more traffic, take note. That's an opportunity to 1) improve that content to get even more traffic, and 2) make sure the content is optimized for your digital marketing funnel (see Chapter 4). Is it linking to the best possible landing page, with a strong call to action? Should it be reshared to more social channels?

You might have done a great job with that content when you published it, but this style of content marketing is a marathon, not a sprint. Months or even years after you publish a piece of content, it might begin to get more traffic. And in the meantime, your business focus may have shifted.

So be mindful of what people are doing and reading on your site, and always look for ways to improve the experience.

The same holds true for social media metrics. It's easy to get caught up in the excitement of large numbers.

Don't.

Instead, work to create relationships with people. Social networks exist to make that as easy as possible, but it's still a person-by-person process.

QUALITATIVE METRICS

You need to be open to whatever the data tells you so you can improve or pivot as needed. That also includes qualitative metrics which, unlike the measurable information from quantitative metrics, is more descriptive and conceptual. Let's take a look at some of the most common examples.

Customer Feedback

One of the best ways to learn about your business and target audience is to . . . wait for it . . . *talk to them!* As lean startup pioneer Steve Blank put it, "Get out of the building."

Make sure you're leaving time and space to talk to your customers and target market. This could be in the form of interviews, focus groups, surveys, and more. We strongly recommend reading *The Lean Startup* by Eric Ries (Crown Publishing Group, 2011) and then *Running Lean: Iterate from Plan A to a Plan That Works* by Ash Maurya (O'Reilly Media, 2010). Together they will give you a perfect understanding of how to start a business lean and how to learn from other people.

By talking to people, you give yourself a unique opportunity to learn and adapt quickly, rather than waiting for monthly, quarterly, or annual reports to discover that something's wrong, and even then not quite knowing what.

Audience Feedback

Along the same lines, make sure you give your audience an opportunity to comment on your blog posts and social content. These comments may sometimes be harsh. If your content is lacking or your message is off, sometimes you need that jolt to see past your own nose.

Comments are also an opportunity to further extend your reach and establish a real community and audience. Inviting email subscribers to reply to you with their questions and comments works the same way.

QUANTITATIVE METRICS

With that understanding of what you're looking for, let's take a closer look at what each of the major networks has to offer. Third-party tools like Agorapulse build on and enhance these reports, but the native platforms are always a good place to begin.

Facebook

As the network that has been servicing businesses the longest, Facebook has the most robust set of available metrics. To access your Page reports, go to your Facebook Page and click on the Insights tab at the top of the screen. You can also go to and even bookmark your Page's facebook.com link followed by /insights/.

The available reports are organized into tabs down the left side and currently include 18 separate reports:

1. Overview
2. Ads
3. Followers
4. Likes
5. Reach
6. Page Views
7. Page Previews
8. Actions on Page
9. Posts
10. Branded Content
11. Events
12. Videos
13. Stories
14. Groups
15. People
16. Messages
17. API
18. Orders

Let's take a look at each of these in greater detail:

- *Overview.* This default tab provides a succinct summary of your Page performance for the past seven days; it can also be adjusted to show today, yesterday, or the last 28 days. It includes a dozen charts for your Page's key metrics for the given time frame, as well as for your five most recent posts. This is also where you can specify a number of other competitors' Facebook Pages and see how your Page measured up.
- *Ads.* The Ads tab remains even though all ad metrics have been moved over to Facebook's Ads Manager. There's literally nothing to see here.
- *Followers.* This series of charts shows how your Page's audience has grown over time, how many are following or unfollowing you, and where that growth is

coming from. The default time frame is the previous 28 days, but you can adjust that using the slider or date range above the charts.

- *Likes.* This series of charts reports Page likes similarly to Followers, above. However, someone who likes your Page is publicly demonstrating their support, and your Page will show up among their liked Pages. Following a Page only subscribes you to that Page's updates. Liking a Page automatically follows a Page, but they can choose to unfollow it if they wish.

- *Reach.* These metrics demonstrate how many people your posts reached, through both paid and organic means, as well as activity like recommendations, reactions, comments, and shares, which can lead to more reach. There is also a chart for hide, report as spam, and unlike, which detract from reach, and then a total reach chart.

- *Page Views.* These charts indicate how much traffic your Facebook Page itself has received for the given time frame, including how many individual people visited the Page and where that traffic came from.

- *Page Previews.* Your page preview is what people see when hovering over your Page name elsewhere on Facebook. One example is on your personal profile, where you might have your business Page listed as your company.

- *Actions on Page.* Every Facebook Page can have a Call to Action button in the lower right corner of its cover photo, as well as several other key actions visitors can take. These include getting directions, clicking through to a website, and tapping on a phone number. These charts reflect what actions your audience took during the given time frame.

- *Posts.* This report shows when your fans are online and engaging with your posts, which post types have performed best during that time frame, and what your competing Pages' top posts were. You can then scroll down to see how every post you made to your Page performed comparatively.

- *Branded Content.* This will open Insights within Facebook's Brand Collabs Manager—a Facebook tool to help facilitate cooperation between your brand and others—(in a new tab) and detail how any posts you had shared and marked as a brand collaboration performed. The benefit to this technique is that all brands involved have shared access to the data.

- *Events.* This will open your Events Manager—the area within Faceobok where you can see and manage all of your events—in a new tab and provide a summary of how your events have performed over the past year, details of active posts, any recommendations from Facebook, and a list of your past events at the bottom. You can review the reach of your events, how many people responded, and potentially how many tickets were sold, if that was an option.

- *Videos.* If you're creating video content for Facebook, this tab is particularly important. It starts by summarizing whether your Page is eligible for in-stream video ads (something to consider if you're looking to monetize your Facebook video content directly), for which you need 10,000 fans and a significant library of existing video content that they are watching. This is followed by a chart demonstrating how many viewing minutes your video content accrued during the given period, how many three-second views, and then all your best videos based on those criteria.
- *Stories.* If you've published Stories to your Page, click through to this tab and turn on Insights for Stories. You'll get a breakdown of how many Stories you've published, how many opens and swipes forward each received, and the total engagement.
- *Groups.* If there's a group linked to your Page, you will have a wonderful set of charts here detailing group membership, active members, posts, comments, reactions, and top contributors. Clicking on More Group Insights will bring you within the group and include membership requests, popular days and popular times.
- *People.* This tab is a useful demographic and geographic breakdown of your Page fans. You can see them by gender split, age ranges, or top countries, cities, and languages.
- *Messages.* These key charts will show you how many messaging connections your Page added in the given time frame and if anyone blocked your Page from messaging them. This is critical if you're using chatbot automation.
- *API.* Unless you're using the API (Application Programming Interface) yourself for a Facebook app, there will be no data here.
- *Orders.* If you have made sales through your Facebook Page, you'll see a tally of those orders here.

Spending some time on these reports, particularly the ones that apply most to the content you're creating for your brand, will provide you with a deep understanding of what's working and what isn't, and help you modify your content-creation strategy moving forward.

LinkedIn

When you go to your LinkedIn Company Page, you actually get a snapshot of your analytics for the past 30 days right there on the first page. It will tell you how many Page visitors you received, change in followers, post impressions, and any clicks on your custom call-to-action button.

Along the top menu bar, you'll see Analytics, which contains three sections: Visitors, Updates, and Followers:

- *Visitors*. These charts show you visitors to your Page over time, whether they were on desktop or mobile, and some fascinating insights into the top job functions of those visitors.
- *Updates*. These charts demonstrate the performance of your Page updates and posts, both paid and organic. You can see the total reactions, comments, and shares; impressions by day broken out by paid or organic; and how each past post performed. If you have added team members to your Company Page, you can see who posted what, and be sure to scroll right when reviewing post performance, as some data columns may be hidden from view.
- *Followers*. Here you'll see your total follower count, how your audience has grown or changed over time, and a very interesting demographics chart breaking down your audience by location, job function, seniority, industry, and company size.

Given that LinkedIn excels at B2B and professional interaction, these metrics can be extremely valuable. Knowing whether your Page updates are reaching your target audience will help inform your future decisions and activities. And all LinkedIn reports can be exported as Excel spreadsheets for further analysis or sharing with colleagues.

YouTube

YouTube, like Facebook, has been working with businesses and creators for some time and therefore has a robust set of metrics. If you go to studio.youtube.com, you'll see a tab for Analytics for your channel in the left-hand menu. Once clicked, you'll have a number of reports across the top to choose from:

- *Overview*. This handy summary report demonstrates video views, watch time, subscribers, and revenue in a series of charts. Note that subscribers are minimally important for YouTube channels, as most people simply watch the videos they need to answer their questions. You can also scroll down to see your top videos during the given time frame and measure real-time activity.
- *Reach*. These are some of the most important charts for your YouTube channel. Impressions tells you how many times your video thumbnails were seen on YouTube, whereas the Impressions clickthrough rate tells you how often users clicked on the thumbnail to view the video. That can tell you a great deal about the effectiveness of your thumbnails, titles, and descriptions. You also get Views and Unique Viewer counts here, and if you scroll down, you can explore where those views came from.

- *Engagement.* How long are your viewers watching your videos? That's what you'll learn here, with total watch time and average duration. You'll also discover your most-watched videos, which ones are receiving the most CTA clicks, best playlists, and more.
- *Audience.* These charts will help you understand how your audience is growing and how much time they're spending on your videos, as well as your demographic and geographic split.
- *Revenue.* If you're monetizing your YouTube channel directly through pre-roll and in-stream ads, these charts will show you estimated earnings for the given time frame, as well as your top-earning videos and ad types.

You can also access more comprehensive versions of all these reports by clicking on See More below each tab's main chart. This will open the complete analytics in an overlay detailing all the earlier tabs, which can be exported into a CSV (comma-separated values, a plain text document) or directly into a Google Sheet.

Instagram

With Instagram firmly entrenched as a mostly mobile experience, it should come as no surprise that its metrics are accessible only through the mobile app. While convenient for those who largely use the app anyway, most businesses who are integrating Instagram into their strategy use a third-party tool for reporting.

To access analytics through the app, open
Instagram and tap your profile icon in the lower right. At the top of the screen under your username, you'll see a brief metric, such as how many visits your profile has received recently. Tap that to access your full profile report. From there you can move to these tabs:

> **TIP**
>
> Note that only business profiles have access to analytics. If you haven't yet switched your profile from personal to business, go into your Settings and do that now to start accruing data.

- *Content.* This tab shows your most recent Stories, posts, and promotions and indicates on each thumbnail how much visibility that content received. Since Stories are only visible to your followers for 24 hours, this is the best way to see how that content performed in the past. Tapping on See All for Content will show you older Stories, posts, and promotions, from as far back as two years ago.
  - If you tap See All for Stories, posts, or promotions, you can change the metric that is displayed on each post from the default Reach setting.
  - Stories can report Back, Calls, Emails, Exited, Follows, Get Directions, Impressions, Link Clicks, Next Story, Profile Visits, Reach, Replies, Shares, Texts, and

Website Clicks. You can view content from the past 24 hours, 7 days, or 14 days.

- Posts can be filtered by Photos, Videos, Carousel Posts, or Shopping Posts, and can display Calls, Comments, Emails, Engagement, Follows, Get Directions, Impressions, Likes, Profile Visits, Reach, Saved, Shares, Texts, and Website Clicks.

- Promotions can report:
  - Visits to profile
  - Number of people who viewed the promotion
  - Number of impressions
  - Number of engagements
  - Audience demographics
  - Amount of money spent

- *Activity.* This tab details by how many accounts (reach) and how many total times (impressions) your content was seen. It shows you only the previous week and compares that with the week before. This is also where you'll find how many times someone viewed your profile directly, as well as clicked through to your website.

- *Audience.* This tab illustrates how your audience has grown over the past week, including a breakdown of follows and unfollows. You can also scroll down to find demographic and geographic splits of your audience, including location, age, gender, and when they tend to be active on Instagram.

Of the networks we've reviewed so far, this is clearly the most limited set of metrics. While not the worst, given Instagram's popularity as a platform for driving brand awareness and engagement, this is a paltry effort. We'll share several options for third-party tools in a moment that will help tremendously.

Twitter

Twitter's reports are perhaps the easiest to use and understand. The initial Analytics overview screen is an excellent place for folks who are new to Twitter analytics to get started. There, you'll find a number of tabs across the top to explore:

- *Home.* The initial overview page is a quick 28-day summary detailing how many tweets, impressions, profile visits, mentions, and followers you accrued, and compares that with the previous period. You can then scroll down through your previous months and see your top tweet, top mention, top follower, and more.

- *Tweets.* This detailed section shows every tweet you shared during the given period, and illustrates your impressions, engagement rate, link clicks, retweets, likes, and replies.

- *Audiences*. This robust set of reports helps you understand your audience breakdown. You can look at your followers or audiences based on specific campaigns. You can explore their interests, occupation, consumer buying styles, wireless carrier, household income, net worth, marital status, education, home ownership, and typical demographic details.

- *Events*. If you're creating events on Twitter, you will see an overview here of all your past events, and then a breakdown by event category (e.g., sports).

- *Videos*. This section shows how many views your videos accumulated over the given period, as well as the completion rate for those videos.

- *App Manager*. If you have a mobile app and are promoting it using Twitter's App Manager, you'll find overview metrics here.

- *Conversion Tracking*. Like Facebook, LinkedIn, and Pinterest, Twitter offers a tracking code, which can be installed on your website and used to track performance. In essence, this will tell you how many times visitors from Twitter "converted" on your site, whether that was a subscription, a download, or a purchase.

Only the Tweets report can be exported, either by tweet or by day.

> **TIP**
>
> Twitter audience data is an estimate based on Twitter partners in the U.S. only. Each section states how much of your audience has been matched and used to generate that statistic (e.g., 15.3 percent).

Pinterest

Pinterest's analytics carry many of the same features and elements as the other networks. The default is the Overview screen, and a drop-down menu in the upper left reveals two other report areas.

- *Overview*. This report starts with a nice summary of your performance over the previous 28 days, including impressions, total audience, engagements, and engaged audience. You can then chart and segment a number of key performance indicators, including:

  1. Impressions
  2. Engagements
  3. Closeups (user tapped to see the pin image larger)
  4. Link clicks
  5. Saves
  6. Engagement rate
  7. Closeup rate

8. Link click rate
9. Save rate
10. Total audience (unique users who viewed your pins)
11. Engaged audience (users who engaged with your pins)

You can also split those insights by content type, claimed accounts, device, source, and format. Below that chart you'll find a carousel that demonstrates your top boards sorted by impressions, engagements, closeups, link clicks, or saves. That's followed by a similar carousel for your top pins.

■ *Audience Insights.* These reports will help you understand the size and composition of your total audience vs. your engaged audience. You can learn their interests and drill down to see more detail, as well as typical demographic and geographic splits.

■ *Video.* If you're uploading video natively to Pinterest, these reports will illustrate the performance of your video content, including views, watch time, link clicks, and saves. The chart can be adjusted to show impressions, link clicks, saves, video views, average watch time, total watch time in minutes, 95 percent views, and ten-second views. These charts can be split much like the pin insights.

Note that all Pinterest reports feature additional filters in the left margin that can apply to all results, similar to the split options for charts.

You can export your Pinterest reports or create a promoted pin campaign targeting an audience segment right from the audience insights section.

While there are many other social networks, some of which have been mentioned in earlier chapters, the ones we've covered in this chapter are the networks that not only have reports available, but are also the platforms on which you are likely active enough to have accumulated meaningful data.

If you're finding success on other networks, we definitely encourage you to explore what, if any, reports those networks offer. Even if they don't provide reports, there are ways in which you can create your own, as we're about to show you.

TOOLS

Whether you're focused on a single social network or have dozens of profiles, third-party tools can make your job and the task of analyzing social media performance and ROI easier and more effective. The following sections focus on some tools that can help you extract the data you need.

Google Sheets

Your best friend throughout this process is going to be Google Sheets. The free, online spreadsheet system is robust enough to handle most reporting needs, can accept imports via CSV and sometimes directly from the platform (e.g., YouTube), and most important, can be shared and downloaded in a variety of ways.

Start a new Google Sheet today and begin entering and tracking the metrics you want to pay attention to. This might be post-performance, audience growth, or ecommerce. You might need to focus on engagement or clickthroughs or video views.

Don't try to track everything; it will be too challenging to focus on anything, unless you're a full-time analyst. Instead, pick out some key metrics you think will give you the best perspective on how you did overall during the given time frame.

There are two added benefits to pulling your metrics into your own spreadsheet (feel free to use Excel or Numbers or another system if you prefer).

First, once you have entered the data, you can now manipulate and calculate it in any way you wish. What was your average post reach last month? How many videos did you upload last quarter? Were there fewer Story exits this month than last month?

Any calculation you want to make is now a simple spreadsheet function applied to a range of cells. You can now also turn that data into one or more graphs—especially useful if you need to communicate results to management or clients!

Second, your own spreadsheet allows you to add extra information, data, or context to what you're entering from a specific social profile. This could include campaign data, categorization, or other business results.

For instance, suppose you crafted a series of Facebook activities that included posts, Story, and video content. Throughout the activities, you referenced an offer on a landing page and used a Google Analytics tracking link to send visitors to the page. With the help of Google Analytics, you can include on your spreadsheet how many people visited your site from those links and what business results occurred—that's measurable ROI!

UTM Parameters and Tracking Links

Tracking links are a vastly underused technique, so it's worth taking the time to review them and include them as a tool.

UTM stands for "Urchin Tracking Module," but trust us, you will never need to remember that. In essence, it's a way for Google to understand a bit more about the link.

Right now, if you share a direct link to your home page in a tweet and someone clicks on it, Google Analytics will record that traffic on your site and automatically label it as coming from Twitter. That's fine for giving you an overall sense of your traffic from that social network, but it is indistinguishable from every other visitor to your home page from Twitter. How do you know someone came to your site from that particular tweet and not from, say, the link in your bio?

Google's UTM allows us to specify *parameters*—aspects of a link we would like to track to differentiate it from other, similar links and traffic. You can choose from a number of parameters, but for our purposes, the three most important are Campaign, Source, and Medium.

1. *Campaign* (utm_campaign): Identifies a specific promotion or campaign.
2. *Source* (utm_source): Indicates where the link and traffic came from.
3. *Medium* (utm_medium): Indicates how that link was shared, such as social network or email.

If those values aren't specified, whenever Google Analytics registers a visit to your site from a link, it will assign Source and Medium whenever possible. You can, however, override those values by including them in the link itself. (In fact, you can put anything you wish in there, so be careful! Misspelling "Twiter" will result in split reports for both versions of the Source.)

To build a link, you simply start with your basic link and add the UTM parameters at the end, creating a longer version of the same link that will still go to the same destination. Like this:

cnn.com ->

cnn.com?utm_source=Guide&utm_medium=Book&utm_campaign=Example

For each parameter you wish to add, start with a "?" immediately after the base URL, add your first parameter, and then add a "&" for each additional parameter. You can only use Campaign if you wish, or any combination of parameters.

Once you begin using tracking links like this, you can view, filter, and adjust your Google Analytics reports to see, for instance, how much traffic came in via specific Campaigns, how much they purchased, and how that activity varied with different Source variables and links you employed.

Of course, those tracking links can get a bit long and, yes, your audience can see the full link, so you may want to take advantage of a link-shortening service like Bitly. You can use a custom domain name so that your links are branded, and even customize the back half of the link to be more meaningful. If I shorten and customize the above tracking link, it can look like this: http://bit.ly/GuideExample.

Pretty neat, huh?

If you want to know how effective your marketing is and how each channel is performing, you must get into the habit of creating tracking links for everything you do.

Agorapulse

There is a *reason* we all use and recommend Agorapulse, and why it's been mentioned several times already throughout this book. It's an all-in-one social media management tool that, among other great features, includes a series of robust, gorgeous reports.

Businesses with Facebook Pages, Twitter profiles, Instagram profiles, and LinkedIn Company Pages can use a single app like Agorapulse to view comprehensive reports for those profiles and then export them for professional documents that can be effectively presented to any manager or client.

Multiple profiles can be combined, adjusted, and filtered to provide just the information you're looking for. So if you don't have time for custom Google Sheets and manual data entry, and want to make a good impression on other stakeholders, Agorapulse is a great option.

Other Tools

If Agorapulse doesn't support the platform you need or isn't a good fit for any other reason, there are many other third-party options available. Here are just a few recommendations:

- *Tailwind.* Tailwind is an excellent platform for Pinterest and Instagram. For Pinterest in particular, the data and insights you can glean are extremely powerful and actionable.
- *Brandwatch.* When you want to learn more about the conversations that are happening online about and around your brand, and want to, for instance, track the performance of a specific hashtag, Brandwatch is a robust option.
- *BuzzSumo.* While this tool focuses on discovering top-performing content and influencers, BuzzSumo's capacity to track that performance over time is an incredible asset, particularly if you're engaging influencers for specific campaigns.

There are many, many other tools out there—one for every need and budget. The key is to notice when you're doing a task repetitively or spending a lot of time on something—chances are there's a tool available to add efficiency and capability.

WHAT'S NEXT

This may have been one of the more overwhelming chapters of the book, so take a breath and give yourself permission to reread it a few times. Depending on your personality and disposition, this much talk of data and numbers and reports may have been very exciting or deeply troubling.

If you're just getting started with your social media efforts and haven't yet done any reporting, start with the Google Sheet method we outlined above. Not only is it free, but forcing yourself to spend a little time every week recording numbers from the platforms you're active on will also teach you awareness and familiarity. You'll get *comfortable* with the data.

It may be tempting to spend your time creating reports that look nice, but you risk detaching yourself from the data. It's more important that your reporting be meaningful and actionable!

But what do you do with that data? How do you change what you're doing based on what the reports are telling you? That's what we're covering in the final chapter. You're almost there!

Chapter 14

Adapt to a Changing Medium

"Build it, and they will come" only works in the movies.
Social media is a "Build it, nurture it, engage them,
and they may come and stay."

—SETH GODIN

This marvelous message from marketing expert Seth Godin is a reference to the 1989 film classic *Field of Dreams*, which starred Kevin Costner as Ray Kinsella, a struggling Iowa farmer who hears an ethereal voice in his cornfield whisper over the wind, "If you build it, he will come."

This is just the first of several messages Ray receives from the voice, leading him through a series of actions, each one crazier than the first.

He plows under half his crops and builds a baseball field in the middle of nowhere. Then he drives to Boston to "ease his pain"—an apparent mission to help a reclusive novelist. The two of them take a trip to Minnesota to "go the distance" and give an elderly man one more shot at his dream. And then ultimately it's revealed who "he" really is and what that person means to Ray.

Now, of course, Seth is absolutely correct when he says that "build it, and they will come" only works in the movies. What we found interesting was the journey the voice asked Ray to take. Rather than skip to the end, he led Ray through a series of steps and tests. Ray *had to learn for himself* how this was all going to work.

What's true for Ray is also true for you and every other business, particularly when it comes to keeping up with changes on social media.

People say that social media changes constantly. They're usually referring to the platforms themselves, and we've said as much already in this book. Every day, on one network or another, a bug is fixed, a feature is added, or something else is changed that completely messes with everyone's sense of normalcy.

But there's more to it than that.

Social media isn't a fast food restaurant where you can order from the same menu day after day. It's more like a busy street in a bustling city, where you might find homes and apartments, shops and schools, parks and churches. At any moment, any number of different people can be found traveling down that avenue, allowing their senses to be assaulted by a thousand contrasting smells and sights and sounds.

Each person there has their own motives and agendas, and they may or may not pay any attention to the other people on the street. And tomorrow's pavement-pounding population will be mostly different. It's a rich and ever-changing tapestry of motion and commotion, filled with wonder and humor, interest and information.

This means even the most boring and robotic of brands will still have a social media presence that changes a *little*. Your post tomorrow will be different from today's, seen by different people at different times of the day, and perceived in completely different ways. This person might share your post while that person might comment.

Every post and every person—every experience and every moment—is completely and utterly unique, which means that social media is truly, constantly in flux.

How then do we keep up with this torrent of change? How do we improve on something today that we know will be different tomorrow?

That's how we're going to wrap up this chapter and this book.

FOLLOW THE PATH

Over the course of the previous 13 chapters, you've learned about the major social networks, the ways in which you can use them, and the specific tactics you can employ, such as video, influencer marketing, paid advertising, and chat automation.

As a result, you should by this point have the beginnings of a marketing plan in progress! If you take notes, by going back through key chapters as necessary, you can pick out the platforms you want to focus on, the strategies you wish to adopt, and the tactics you believe you should employ.

With this plan in hand, you now have a path to take. Like any journey, taking that first step is the key. Without a plan and a concerted effort to follow and execute it, you'll have nothing to iterate or improve upon.

So start there.

Choose the network or networks you're going to focus on first, and create the activity and engagement we've been talking about throughout these pages. Begin to connect with a broader audience, all the while keeping your eyes and ears tuned to the individual customer, who can inform you better than anyone how your products, services, and messaging are resonating.

TAKE A BEAT

Once you start this journey, you need to allow yourself and your brand (and your marketing) time. You must give every strategy and tactic sufficient time to have an impact and create enough measurable data to be judged. But also make sure you *are* measuring the activities and results that matter so you can tell when things go off the rails.

It's a fine line, and there's no universal answer for *how much time*?

First, let's be honest: Your initial posts and social media activity will be horrid. Mike's first blog post was wretched. Stephanie's first video was a hot mess. Amanda's first ad bombed, and Jenn's first Instagram post . . . well, OK, maybe Jenn was amazing from the start.

But most people need time to get good at things!

They say it takes 10,000 hours to become an expert at a skill. While you definitely do not need to become a marketing expert, you *will* need to achieve a level of competency for it to be effective. That will take time and practice and repetition.

Second, even the best marketing activity relies on other people seeing it to work. As you ramp up your social media activity and create opportunities for more people to follow and engage with you, your audience will grow.

Slowly. Over time.

Unless you have personal celebrity status or a brand with a household name, creating a new social profile and building an audience will take a while. On both counts, be patient with yourself, your team, and your plan.

HAVE A GO

Once you've started executing a thoughtful and documented marketing plan, you will have opportunities to start testing ideas and theories. This can actually be a lot of fun, and help keep your marketing activities fresh and interesting to yourself and your audience.

Through testing, you can learn definitively what works and what doesn't. This is how you will iterate and improve your marketing (a technique you can employ in other areas of your business as well).

Following the scientific method helps tremendously here. It starts with establishing a hypothesis, or a question. This might take the form of wondering whether a particular technique might work for you and your audience. Or asking whether you should take this or that approach.

Here are some things you might test on different networks:

- Cover images on Facebook, Twitter, YouTube, or LinkedIn
- Post image content/perspective/type
- Post copy length/content
- Tone/style/voice
- Thumbnail images on YouTube
- Hashtags
- Audience targeting
- Timing/frequency
- Objectives
- Mentions and tags
- Cross-promotion
- Employee advocacy
- Brand partnerships
- Automation
- Video, video, video

In addition to testing different tactics on channels you are already active on, consider entirely new channels as tests in themselves!

Scientific Testing

It may be tempting to get excited about the potential of what all the channels and tactics can do for your business. Be patient with this, too. You need to give yourself time to become remarkable at any given tactic, and the more you have going on at once, the more challenging it becomes to know what's working.

And that's the crux of the scientific method: You form a hypothesis and then test that by eliminating as many variables as possible. The Social Media Lab at Agorapulse does this every single week with new blog posts and podcasts revealing the results of experiments they've run.

Unfortunately, the nature of social media means it's technically impossible to run a truly controlled scientific experiment. However, the more effort you put into considering, tracking and recording, and then analyzing the results, the more informed your decisions will be.

Mile Markers

Before you make any change of significance, annotate your Google Analytics (navigate to any report over time and click on +Create New Annotation to add a simple note). You might also comment on your Google Sheets or put a note in your calendar. Do *something* to track when a change is made so you can easily check the date when analyzing for any impact said change may have had. All too often we neglect this crucial step and then are left to guess when we did something that we want to measure the results from.

Benchmarks

This is also a good time to put proper benchmarks in place. If you're using the reports and analytics we reviewed previously, you'll have built-in benchmarks against *yourself*. Now take note of your competitors or other brands of interest in your industry, vertical, or even geographical region, and benchmark them.

With Facebook it's easy, since you can watch their Page performance within your own Page Insights. If you're interested in brands on other networks, you can start another Google Sheet for their key metrics, or use a tool like Agorapulse or SEMrush that includes competitor monitoring.

Split Testing

When possible, split test.

A split test or "A/B test" is when you create two versions of something—say, an image—with one key aspect that differs. When you share the images, you use the same text and everything else that you can reasonably duplicate. Then measure the results and see which version did better with your audience.

You can consider testing additional aspects—known as multivariate testing—but it's a little more complicated. If you have a sufficient audience size and want to test three versions of an image, you can do that. If you wanted to test two images and two different versions of text, you'd actually need to run four posts—one for each combination of image and text—and then compare the results.

It can get pretty complicated!

Regardless of whether you keep it simple or enjoy weaving tangled webs of variation, the goal is to administer a test that results in data-driven, actionable advice, such as "Use more images with happy people" or "Use these hashtags in future posts."

The split test results tell you which version is best, but that also means the winning asset or tactic should now perform better than what you were using before. You will have improved in a statistically measurable way.

Using these methods and some of the other ideas outlined above, you can create all kinds of tests to help you learn about your business and improve your marketing. But how else can you level up your brand?

GET ON BOARD

Routinely spend time educating yourself and your team on current best practices. What are the strategies, tactics, apps, and platforms that other brands are succeeding with today? How can you leverage that knowledge to create new opportunities for your own brand?

You can:

- Read more books like this one
- Attend webinars
- Go to conferences, meetups, and events
- Subscribe to podcasts
- Watch weekly live video shows
- Join relevant Facebook groups
- Join relevant LinkedIn groups
- Participate in weekly Twitter chats
- Follow LinkedIn Influencers
- Subscribe to industry blogs
- Subscribe to industry YouTube channels

Pick a few of the above methods and some specific experts to follow to keep that saw sharpened. That will help you tremendously, but there's one technique most books and gurus don't talk about that may be the most effective thing you can do to help yourself and your business:

Form a board of advisors or mastermind group.

A *board of advisors* is typically a diverse group of professionals with a range of business experience, who you can turn to for advice and answers. A *mastermind* is a small group of peers and colleagues who meet regularly to share how their professional lives are progressing and offer one another support and encouragement.

You can choose to create these groups formally or informally, and build one or both models—what's important is that you have a network of people to whom you can turn for help when you need it. When it comes to social media marketing, either group can give you feedback on what you're doing and fill you in on campaigns they've seen or participated in.

As we mentioned in Chapter 1, Amanda, Mike, Jenn, and Stephanie have a mastermind group, where we regularly share what we're working on, what we hope to accomplish, or what we're struggling with. We have a private Facebook group for sharing longer posts or important information, and a group Messenger chat for quick questions or updates.

Take a moment to think about whom you might reach out to when creating a board of advisors or mastermind group of your own. Your future self will thank you for it!

CORRECT THE COURSE

So far, we've been talking about testing tactics, learning about what's new in social media marketing, and getting information and guidance from your peers.

But what do you do when it feels like nothing is working at all? Where do you turn when your marketing *fails*?

Failure is OK. You can learn a lot from failing! Social media posts that bomb teach you what your audience *isn't* interested in.

But one post that crashes and burns isn't really a "failure." What about when it's an entire campaign or initiative or channel? In that instance, it's critical to look for successes, no matter how small they may be, and use the experience to inform and pivot your social media marketing.

For instance, suppose you tried a live video series and just couldn't get any traction at all. If after a dozen or more shows you still weren't getting any new viewers or increase in business, clearly the tactic is not working and needs to be reevaluated.

But it's still not a total loss.

You've aired more than a dozen live videos online, which means you're better at live video now than you were when you started. That's valuable experience you can apply to later campaigns. And while you may not have gotten many viewers, you still have a library of video content. Can it be repurposed for other channels? Can you build on what you learned in this series and try something else—either a different show format or a different platform?

Sometimes we have to listen to what our customers and our gut are telling us. The experts and your research may have said you should use X strategy on Y network, but if it's just not working after several months, it's OK to try something else.

It's often said that we're our own worst critics, and it's true. We scrutinize our decisions and actions with the power of an electron microscope, failing to realize that no one has that same depth of perspective and interest.

Self-analysis is important, and sometimes change, even dramatic change, is necessary. But every change you make is an opportunity to grow and prosper in ways you couldn't anticipate.

From 2012 to 2018, Mike published thousands of blog posts on social media marketing, email marketing, SEO, and blogging. But when he looked at the data, he found that a hundred articles on blogging he'd published in that span were getting virtually no traffic. He took a chance and moved all those posts to their own website. Those posts now get more traffic in a day than they did over an entire quarter on the old site!

And for years, Amanda worked to build a business and brand centered on all things social media. Frustrated with her lack of growth, she rebranded herself The Digital Gal in 2019 and focused her content and services on social advertising and chat automation. As a result, her reputation and business soared!

The one constant here is change. Networks change. People change. Your business and marketing strategy will change. So what we're going to do here at the end of the book is *reframe* that change. Instead of trying to hold fast to a concept that's fleeting at best, let's embrace change and be excited about it.

Changes to social media marketing can be fun and exciting opportunities for tremendous business growth. They can be challenging, but also thought-provoking. They can consume precious time, but they can also allow us to invest our time wisely, while our competition does not.

Change can actually help you differentiate yourself from your competition—or, rather, your *acceptance* of change can. While the business down the street stubbornly continues to post six times a day to a Facebook Page that's no longer reaching anyone, you, armed with your newfound knowledge and change-focused motivation, can happily pursue more effective tactics and WIN at marketing and business!

Congratulations! You've reached the end of the *Ultimate Guide to Social Media Marketing*, but this is just the beginning of your larger journey. You have an expanse of opportunity in front of you, filled with compelling conversations and campaigns.

Get after it!

Resources

Here are useful tools and resources referenced throughout the book that can help you with all aspects of your social media and digital marketing.

EDITING IMAGES

Canva: https://www.canva.com/

Easil: https://about.easil.com/

Photoshop: https://www.adobe.com/products/photoshop.html

SOCIAL MEDIA BLOGS AND BLOGGERS

Andrew & Pete: https://www.andrewandpete.com/

Andrew Davis: https://www.akadrewdavis.com/

The Digital Gal: https://thedigitalgal.com/

Peg Fitzpatrick: https://pegfitzpatrick.com/

Jenn's Trends: https://www.jennstrends.com/

Lights, Camera, Live: https://www.lightscameralive.com/

Donna Moritz: https://sociallysorted.com.au/

Rebekah Radice: https://rebekahradice.com/

Razor Social: https://www.razorsocial.com/

Mark Schaefer: https://businessesgrow.com/

Neal Schaffer: https://nealschaffer.com/

Social Media Examiner: https://www.socialmediaexaminer.com/

The Social Media Hat: https://www.thesocialmediahat.com/

Social Media Lab: https://www.agorapulse.com/social-media-lab/

SOCIAL MEDIA COMMUNITIES

The Blogging Brute Squad: https://www.facebook.com/groups/bloggingbrutesquad/

Jenn's Trends in Social Media: https://www.facebook.com/groups/1914407545476748/

Social Media Strategist: https://www.facebook.com/groups/smstrategist/

SOCIAL MEDIA MANAGEMENT TOOLS

Agorapulse: https://www.agorapulse.com/

Buffer: https://buffer.com/

Hootsuite: https://hootsuite.com/

Later: https://later.com/

Plann: https://www.plannthat.com/

Sprout Social: https://sproutsocial.com/

Tailwind: https://www.tailwindapp.com/

SOURCING IMAGES

Depositphotos: https://depositphotos.com/

iStock: https://www.istockphoto.com/

Pixabay: https://pixabay.com/

Shutterstock: https://www.shutterstock.com/

FOR MORE READING

Berger, Jonah. *Contagious: Why Things Catch On*. New York: Simon & Schuster, 2013.

Handley, Ann. *Everybody Writes: Your Go-To Guide to Creating Ridiculously Good Content*. Hoboken, NJ: Wiley, 2014.

Kawasaki, Guy, and Peg Fitzpatrick. *The Art of Social Media: Power Tips for Power Users*. New York: Portfolio, 2014.

Schaffer, Neal. *The Age of Influence: The Power of Influencers to Elevate Your Brand*. Nashville, TN: HarperCollins Leadership, 2020.

Scott, David Meerman. *The New Rules of Marketing and PR: How to Use Social Media, Online Video, Mobile Applications, Blogs, News Releases & Viral Marketing to Reach Buyers Directly*. Hoboken, NJ: Wiley, 2017.

Glossary

about. Virtually every social network includes a space where a user can say something about themselves. The amount of available space varies, from the 160 characters in the Twitter bio to the 2,000 characters in LinkedIn's profile summary. Sometimes referred to as a *bio*.

Advanced Audio Coding (AAC). A common audio file compression format.

advertising. A mechanism through which businesses can pay to reach social network users with platform-specific content and media. Advertisers are typically charged per user action, where an "action" might be visiting a website, following a profile, or engaging with content.

advisory board. A group of professionals, typically representing different business interests, who can give you useful advice.

album. A collection of images shared together to Facebook.

alt tag. The alternative text for an image on a web page used by search engines.

analytics. Reports that share collections of data points for a specific date range. For social networks, this typically includes follower growth, post reach and engagement, and audience demographics.

Android. The operating system for smartphones from brands like Google or Samsung.

application (app). A program for a mobile device or computer that is used to provide functionality and create a more immersive experience than a typical website.

artificial intelligence. A term used to describe the ability of a computer system and application to "learn" and adjust based on users and user activity.

aspect ratio. The ratio of an image's width to its height; e.g., 16:9.

audiogram. Technically a video, the audiogram typically uses voice recording, such as a podcast, and static imagery or wave visualization combined into a video media format.

augmented reality. A system by which a user can visualize their environment overlaid with additional visual elements and information.

authenticity. Portraying a personality on social media that is an accurate reflection of who you are as a person and brand.

bio. See *about*.

blog. A collection of articles on a website, organized in reverse chronological order. An individual article published to the blog is called a post or blog post.

board. A predefined collection on Pinterest to which you can save content.

bps. A measurement of the speed of digital communication, which stands for "bits per second."

brand awareness. How many people know about a particular brand and are familiar with what it does.

broadcast. See *live video*.

Business Page. See *Facebook Page* or *LinkedIn Company Page*.

campaign. Within social media advertising, the top level of ad organization. More generally, campaigns are organized marketing initiatives that can include social media, content, and more, designed to achieve a specific goal.

carousel. When multiple images are posted to Instagram or shared within the same ad unit, allowing viewers to scroll through the images.

chat. A form of instant text communication that takes place within a social platform. Chat typically includes status indicators and other real-time features.

chatbot. Services are available to automate responses to questions and comments from chat participants. These workflows and automations are collectively referred to as a chatbot.

click. Usually refers to a social network user clicking on a link within a post or ad that leads to an external website. Can also include clicking on an image or video to see or view more, clicking through to a profile, clicking to download an app, and other nonengagement actions.

clickthrough rate. Out of the total number of people who viewed a post or ad, the number who clicked the link to visit the associated website.

comment. Most social media and blog posts allow readers and audience members to write some kind of response, such as feedback or a question. Comments are usually text, but in some instances can include images, stickers, or even video.

community. Often used synonymously with groups, it can also refer to the larger body of fans and followers that compose a brand's audience, either on a specific network or overall.

connect. A two-way, mutually accepted relationship between two social network users.

content. While typically used in reference to website content, such as blog posts or landing pages, in a broader sense it can also include text, images, and video shared to social media or even sent through email.

content marketing. The discipline and approach to marketing that incorporates web-based content, social media marketing, and email marketing to drive traffic and use content to educate and funnel prospects.

conversion. When a website visitor or social media follower takes a desired action, such as making a purchase.

cover photo. Some networks like Facebook allow users to customize their profile by uploading a large image that runs across the top of the profile.

crosspost. When a Facebook Page broadcasts a live video, that video can be simultaneously broadcast on partner Pages. Such broadcasts are treated as natively live videos on all participating Pages, which all share the same video metrics.

dark social media. A variety of ways in which users can share your content and information privately on social media, making it invisible to you. Direct messages are an example.

demographic. Basic user information, such as age and gender. Some networks can identify additional data, such as job title or income.

direct message (DM). A private one-to-one messaging system between users of a network. Most social networks offer some form of direct message.

ebook. A digital document, usually in PDF format, that provides extensive information and can be easily distributed or offered in exchange for an email address.

email. Electronic distribution of messages over a computer network.

email marketing. The use of email to promote new content, share business opportunities, and generally talk about your business and other topics of interest directly to individual subscribers.

embed. Taking an external element like a social post or video and inserting it into your web page or blog post so that readers can see it without needing to go to its original location. Most social networks provide code with each post so they can easily be embedded.

engagement. When a social network user chooses to take an available action on a post, such as like, comment, or share. Most commonly associated with individual posts.

engagement rate. The rate at which viewers of a post or video engaged with it, calculated by dividing the number of engagements by the number of unique viewers.

event. A calendared post that can be about an online or offline activity. Facebook and LinkedIn support event posts that have unique features, such as ticket sales or invitations.

Facebook. A social network launched in 2004 that focuses on personal connections.

Facebook group. A community within Facebook that can be public or private, containing two or more members.

Facebook Live. A live video broadcast to a Facebook profile, Page, or group.

Facebook Messenger. A messaging app produced by Facebook that allows users to send text messages, send multimedia files including photos and videos, and make voice and video calls.

Facebook Page. A business profile on Facebook that includes additional features such as analytics.

Facebook Watch. The area within Facebook reserved for video content, particularly episodic shows.

favorite. Some networks refer to their post reaction as a favorite. Formerly on Twitter, users could see all tweets that they had marked in this way.

Flickr. A social network focused on uploading unique photo content.

follow. A one-way, nonmutual relationship between two social network users.

follower. A social network user who has formally liked or followed your profile.

friend. A Facebook user with whom you have agreed to connect.

Friendster. One of the early social networks; no longer active.

funnel. A visualization of the journey prospects take through the sales or marketing process, as they move toward a decision and purchase.

geographic. Specific cities, regions, states, and countries that users log in from, typically obtained through analyzing their internet connection.

geolocation tag. Geographic location metadata added to a photo or video.

Google. The most popular search engine, and one of the most valuable brands in the world.

Google+. A social network based on social circles and communities of interest; created by Google, but no longer active.

Google Analytics. A free reporting system provided by Google that identifies and measures website visitor traffic, patterns, and results.

Google My Business. A collection of services, primarily for local businesses, which help inform potential customers of a business's location, hours, reviews, and more.

Graphics Interchange Format (GIF). An image format that incorporates a brief series of frames to simulate video.

group. A mechanism provided by some social networks that allows two or more users to form a community, typically offering group-specific communication features.

hashtag. Text preceded by a pound sign (#), which can be a single word or a long phrase without spaces. When included in a social network post, that post will appear in the results whenever a user performs a search for that hashtag.

image. A visual element, which is typically in a JPEG, PNG, or GIF format.

image post. A share of one or more images directly to a social network.

impressions. The number of times a post was viewed, potentially including multiple views by the same user.

influencer. An individual who has built an audience, of any size, who are interested in that influencer and the topics they commonly discuss; they have thus shown they can be influenced by that person.

influencer marketing. The calculated use of influencers to reach their audience and potentially persuade them to take a business action as a direct result of their trust in the influencer.

insights. See *analytics*.

Instagram. A social network launched in 2010 that focuses on sharing image content.

Instagram TV (IGTV). Instagram's dedicated section, and stand-alone app, for viewing video content.

interests. Additional information gleaned about users based on actions they've taken within a platform (such as following a brand), and made available as targeting options to advertisers on networks like Facebook, Twitter, Instagram, and Pinterest.

iOS. The operating system for Apple iPhones, iPads, and Watches.

JPEG. A common image file compression format created by the Joint Photographic Experts Group in 1992.

like. The iconic action Facebook created to give users a mechanism for reacting to individual posts. Users can also like a Facebook Page.

link. A permanent address to a website or content within a website that can be shared and clicked on to take the user to that web page.

link post. When a link is shared to a social network, that network creates a link post. Typically this includes drawing information from the linked page, including title, description, and image, if available.

link preview. When a link post is created and the website has specified title, description, and image, the social network will create a card with that information for the link.

LinkedIn. A social network launched in 2003 that focuses on business relationships.

LinkedIn Company Page. A profile page for businesses within LinkedIn that includes specific functionality for businesses, including analytics.

LinkedIn Live. A feature that allows users to broadcast live video on LinkedIn.

list. Some networks like Twitter offer the ability to segment connections or followers into private groups for ease of management.

live video. Several social networks allow users to broadcast video in real time, including the use of third-party applications that can facilitate features like additional guests, alternate camera angles, graphic overlays, and more.

location. Used for audience targeting, either on specific posts or in advertisements, based on geographic data.

Maslow's hierarchy of needs. A psychological theory created by Abraham Maslow that classifies human behavioral needs from the most basic to the most complex: physiological, safety, belonging and love, esteem, and self-actualization.

mastermind group. A collection of peers and colleagues who regularly meet and support one another.

mention. When posting or commenting on a social network, typing another user's name in such a way that they are notified by the network. This is typically accomplished by typing an @ symbol in front of their name.

Messenger. See *Facebook Messenger*.

Messenger marketing. The use of the Messenger platform and chatbot automation to reach and leverage social network users more directly.

metadata. Data that describes other data.

Midwest Digital Marketing Conference (MDMC). A significant social media conference that is held in St. Louis, Missouri, each spring.

MOV. A common multimedia file format produced by Apple Inc. for Windows and macOS platforms.

MP4. A common format for storing multimedia files compressed with the MPEG-4 compression algorithm.

MPEG. A common video file compression algorithm produced by the Moving Picture Experts Group. The current standard is MPEG-4.

MySpace. One of the early social networks that has since changed focus to the entertainment industry.

notification. An alert from a social network indicating something has happened that requires your attention, such as a comment on one of your posts.

online marketing. An umbrella term that includes social media marketing, content, SEO, email, paid advertising, and more.

paid social media. See *advertising*.

pay-per-click (PPC). A method of paying for advertising based on the number of clickthroughs.

Periscope. A social network owned by and integrated with Twitter that focuses on live video.

permalink. Every social network post can be linked to directly from outside that network. That "permanent link" can typically be found by right-clicking on the post's date stamp.

Photoshop. An image editing app designed and produced by Adobe Inc.

pin. An image (with or without a link) shared to a Pinterest board.

Pinterest. A social network launched in 2010 that focuses on "how-to" content.

pixel (image). The smallest unit of a digital image displayed and represented on a screen.

pixel (social media). A snippet of code installed within your website to enable audience tracking for social networks.

playlist. A user-specified list of videos.

podcast. Audio-based content available for download via iTunes, Google Play, and Spotify, which is usually episodic in nature.

Portable Network Graphics (PNG). A common image compression format created in 1996 and designed as an improvement of and replacement for the GIF.

post. A share of some kind to social media that can be seen by other users.

private message (PM). See *direct message (DM)*.

profile. An individual's account on a social network and the information that represents that individual, such as a *profile photo* or *about*.

profile photo. An image that represents you and your profile, which is typically attached to your post activity on a social network.

Quora. A social network founded in 2009 that focuses on asking and answering questions.

reach. The number of unique individuals who viewed a particular post or ad.

reaction. Facebook and LinkedIn have expanded the ways an individual can interact with a post to include additional sentiments beyond "like."

Reddit. A social network founded in 2005 that focuses on sharing links and images.

remarketing. The ability to target users with advertising based on a history of activity, such as website visits.

reply. A comment on a tweet.

repurpose. To take one piece of content, such as a video, and change it into a different piece of content, such as a podcast.

retargeting. See *remarketing*.

return on investment (ROI). A calculation of how much business revenue was generated as the result of an activity or set of activities and their business cost.

retweet. A share of a tweet, with or without additional text commenting on it.

search engine. A website that indexes and ranks other websites and makes the results available to people looking for information.

search engine optimization (SEO). Improving a website's ranking in search engines through updating and changing the content, backlinks, and other factors.

share. Taking an existing social media post and sending it to your own feed so your audience can see it.

Six Degrees. An early social network founded in 1997 that no longer exists.

SlideShare. A social network founded in 2006 that focuses on sharing presentations and documents.

Snapchat. A social network launched in 2011 that focuses on conversations deleted after 24 hours.

social media. The set of online platforms and networks that individuals and businesses around the world use to communicate with one another in a variety of ways, based on long-term connections.

Social Media Day. Celebrated on June 30 each year, the event is often marked by conferences and meetups in major cities.

social media management tool. An application that is used to accomplish specific tasks for one or more social networks without requiring the user to interact with that network directly. This may include publishing posts, scheduling activity, monitoring comments, or reporting results.

social media marketing. A coordinated effort to market a brand or organization through social media.

Social Media Marketing World (SMMW). A significant conference that takes place in San Diego, California, each spring.

social network. A social media website that allows users to create accounts and offers social networking features such as connect, post, or comment.

sticker. Clip art that can be used on certain social networks (e.g., Facebook) in comments, posts, Stories, and chat.

Story. A vertical post format originating on Snapchat but now duplicated in other platforms like Facebook, Instagram, and YouTube, it can be an image or video and is automatically removed after 24 hours.

strategy. A plan of action with a specific goal in mind.

stream or streaming. See *live video*.

subscribe. A type of following specific to networks like YouTube that includes notifying users of new content.

SWOT analysis. A business self-assessment that stands for strengths, weaknesses, opportunities, and threats.

tactic. A specific action meant to support an overall strategy.

tag. On some social networks, posted images can include tags that indicate and link to specific users on those networks.

targeting. Identifying in a post or ad a specific segment of users that can see it.

text post. A post to a social network that contains only text.

thumbnail. A small version of an image. Also refers to the initial still frame of videos on YouTube, often customized to include the video's title or other useful information.

TikTok. A social network launched in 2017 that focuses on video sharing.

tweet. A post on Twitter.

Twitter. A social network launched in 2006 that focuses on sharing brief text content.

Twitter chat. An organized conversation on Twitter where every tweet must include a specified hashtag, typically lasting 30 to 60 minutes each week.

unfollow. To choose to stop following a user or brand on a social network.

unfriend. To choose to discontinue a Facebook connection with another user.

Uniform Resource Locator (URL). See *link*.

Urchin Tracking Module (UTM) parameters. Tracking parameters that can be added to a link to give Google Analytics additional context.

video. Multimedia files that can be shared to certain social networks.

video post. A share of a video file to social networks.

Vine. A social network that focused on six-second looping videos; it is no longer active.

vlog. Short for video blog, a vlog is a website hosting a collection of videos, organized in reverse chronological order.

Watch Party. A feature within Facebook that allows users to invite others to watch one or more prechosen videos together as though they were being broadcast live.

WhatsApp. A social network founded in 2009 that focuses on real-time chat.

Yelp. A social network founded in 2004 that focuses on sharing reviews of local businesses.

YouTube. A social network launched in 2005 that focuses on sharing video content.

YouTube channel. A profile on YouTube where a user can upload videos and organize them into playlists.

About the Authors

ERIC BUTOW

Eric Butow is the owner of Butow Communications Group (BCG) in Jackson, California. BCG offers website design, online marketing, and technical writing services for businesses. Eric founded BCG in 1994 specializing in graphic design, and soon offered technical writing and web design services as well.

After Eric graduated from California State University, Fresno in 1996 with a master's degree in communications, he moved to Roseville, California, and continued to build his business. He worked with a wide variety of businesses from startups to large companies including Adobe, Cisco Systems, HP, and Intel.

Eric began his book authoring career by writing *Master Visually Windows 2000 Server* in 2000. Since then, Eric has written 34 more technical books as an author, co-author, or, in one case, as a ghostwriter. Eric's most recent books are *Programming Interviews for Dummies* (Wiley), *Pro iOS Security and Forensics* (Apress), and *Instagram for Business for Dummies* (Wiley).

JENN HERMAN

Jenn Herman is a social media consultant, speaker, and globally recognized Instagram expert. She is the forefront blogger on Instagram marketing and her blog, *Jenn's Trends*, has won the title of a Top 10 Social Media Blog in 2014, 2015, and 2016.

Through her blog, consulting, and speaking, Jenn provides tips, resources, and training for small- to medium-sized businesses that need to structure their social media strategies. Her business background includes Administration, Sales, Human Resources, and Marketing, and she enjoys bringing all these skills together to help you grow your business.

Jenn has been featured in Inc., Fox News, Yahoo Finance, CBS Radio LA, and numerous other podcasts and publications. She is the author of *Instagram for Business for Dummies*, *The Ultimate Beginner's Guide to Instagram* and *Stop Guessing: Your Step-by-Step Guide to Creating a Social Media Strategy*.

STEPHANIE LIU

Stephanie Liu is one of the most sought-after international speakers on live video, known for her dynamic stage presence and cutting-edge Facebook engagement tactics.

She led paid search advertising for one of the largest search agencies in the United States, served as the Director of Social Strategy for San Diego's leading ad agency, and has created powerful campaigns for small businesses to giant, multimillion-dollar corporations. As a digital marketing strategist, she spent a decade deep in the trenches of agency life where her experience opened doors to working with big brand names such as Coach, Givenchy, Nike, and Sony Pictures Entertainment. Her work has been recognized and awarded by Online Marketing Media and Advertising (OMMA) and PR Daily.

Stephanie is most notably known for her Facebook Live show called Lights, Camera, Live®, where she helps businesses succeed with live video.

AMANDA ROBINSON

Amanda Robinson is the founder of *The Digital Gal*. She is widely sought after in the digital marketing industry for her knowledge and experience as a Facebook Ads expert. She advises Social Media Examiner's membership group, the Social Media Marketing Society, with over 2,000 entrepreneurs and digital marketers. She is regularly featured as a guest on digital marketing podcasts and speaks both on stage and in workshop settings on everything from Facebook Ads to Analytics to Messenger Marketing Chatbots.

In recent projects, Amanda was a key player in #RoadToSocial, a Social Media Road trip across the U.S. Midwest covering three back-to-back digital marketing conferences with 1.9M reach and 20.3M impressions on the #RoadToSocial content.

Amanda's real flair for digital marketing comes with her hands-on experience with extreme deep dives into data analysis focusing on analytics, SEO, ad targeting, split testing, and ways to make your marketing dollars more efficient.

MIKE ALLTON

Mike is a Content Marketing Practitioner—a title he invented to represent his holistic approach to content marketing that leverages blogging, social media, email marketing and SEO to drive traffic, generate leads, and convert those leads into sales.

He is an award-winning blogger, speaker, and author at *The Social Media Hat*, and Brand Evangelist at Agorapulse.

As Brand Evangelist, Mike works directly with other social media educators, influencers, agencies, and brands to explore and develop profitable relationships with Agorapulse.

Index